Gimme Some Relationship Advice!

How to Find Love and Keep it

Bayyinah Monk - Nduaka

This book is dedicated
to my darling love, best friend, soul mate - husband,
Obinna C. Nduaka. His love and strength inspires me.
And to the beautiful people looking to
attract a healthy
love; and to those maintaining a healthy love,
may your love thrive eternally.

Contents

Preface

Late night talks with the girls, disagreements, learning through watching others mistakes, bad choices, heartbreaks, sad days and love disappointments is what drove me to write a relationship book. This relationship book has been in development for a couple years now. With nervousness in their voices, I was often asked by my friends, family and peers if their names would be mentioned in this relationship book. Amusingly and jokingly, I said Yes! Honestly this book is written for everyone out there looking for a love, and trying to keep a love. I like to believe that all my experiences in life whether it was through previous relationships or in my other paths in life have all contributed to who I am today.

In the movie Vampire in Brooklyn, Eddie Murphy compares how two opposites – good and bad have to work hand in hand in order to exist. You have to have dark in order to have light...If every day is a sunny day, then what's a sunny day?

You have to have dark in order to have light. Trials in life are often preparations or training for your future position in life. To prepare you for something good. If you are tired and feel like you are "doing all the right things" but still end up with emotional manipulators or toxic relationships who are unable to show a healthy love, it is best to make happiness your priority and becoming a whole you before seeking a new love. Ultimately, it's your choice, it's your commitment decision. In order for the advice in this book to be successful, you must be committed to the steps and the process in attracting a healthy love. If you are reading this book, my desire is for you to be prepared and reading this with an opened mind and open heart to make the necessary changes needed.

Over all, gaining clarity on why people do some of the things they do can help move in a better direction to finding a healthy love, and keeping it alive. And that's what you will find in this book. I pray that you find and attract a healthy love that may grow and flourish. You deserve it!

~Bayyinah Monk-Nduaka

Introduction

What Is Love?

Where there is love, there is life.
-Mahatma Gandhi

What constitutes love has been attempted to be defined by many over the years. It has been attempted to be defined through both sexes - man and woman; by therapists, philosophers, analysts and as individuals we have all attempted to fully define what constitutes love. The Merriam-Webster dictionary defines love as "a feeling of strong or constant affection or attachment for a person".

Going back into ancient times, the Egyptians drew love poems that were composed thousands of years ago in the form of hieroglyphics symbols which were found in the pyramids and tombs. The Greeks defined love and took it a step further to break the definition down into four categories: Eros – physical sexual desire; Philos – brotherly love which is affection one would have for "charity" not getting anything in return; Storge – love for a family like love, the need to have affection and lastly; Agape – a love that is unconditional, whether you are pleased or not pleased.

Whether we may not all agree on the micro definitions of love - but ultimately, we can all agree that love is an unconditional and endearing set of emotions towards someone you are close to. It can include a parent's love to a child, or the connection to a man or a woman.   Although we may never truly define or agree on what love truly is, we can identify and list the things that *love is not*. Love is not: impatient, being used, being abused, unforgiving, disrespectful, hurtful, mean, manipulative, dishonest, disloyal. Love include: being understanding, happy, loyal, caring, giving, dear, flexible, patient, kind, humble, forgiving. Love is all these things and can be defined as more.

Love as a Psychological Need

Food, shelter and clothing. We have been taught that these are the three basic human needs in order to survive. They are vital and essential for humans to survive. Taking it one step further, what if I told you that love was also needed to survive? Love is needed and yearned for in order to survive and thrive throughout life.

In Maslow's Hierarchy of Needs, a psychological theory that tiers human needs expressed in a pyramid, it expresses that love and attachment comes in the middle as third on the pyramid right after the basic needs of 1. food, shelter, and clothing; and 2. safety and security. The pyramid is meant to be read from the bottom up, with the bottom being the most important needs in order to survive.

In order to have our psychological needs met to survive as humans, it is imperative to have love, a sense of belonging and attachment. Love can be defined as "an intense feeling of warmth and attachment or of deep affection".

When a mother give birth to a child, the very first thing is for the child to latch on and suck from mother's breast; this is a natural display of affection and closeness. Once a child continues to grow, there is a critical period of brain development from birth up until about they are kindergarten age, during this time, loving, affection and physical contact is very important for the normal growth and development of the child. If the child is not loved, cuddled, held or hugged, then the child's growth may suffer impairment or stunting, and the child's brain may not mature properly.

Research shows that children who grew up in orphanages, and did not receive love and affection; who were only fed and cleaned, showed severe developmental and cognitive delays and even some permanent damage to their brainwaves. Later in life, the child may grow up without having the ability to love or make emotional attachments, and can later lead to patterns of having bad friendships and unhealthy relationships.

Some doctors have done studies with their patients and realized that their patients who received regular visits from friends and family tend to live longer, while those who are alone without any visitors, tend to die sooner.

Deep within us all, we have a yearning to love and to be loved and a desire to feel connected. It was an emotional dynamic ingrained in us all as babies coming out of our mother's womb. Love is not only needed for a good quality of life and well-being, but it is said to have immense impact on the keys to longer living, maintaining good health and succeeding. Love is a strong driving force, sort of like a magnetic force. Some people are willing to do many things to be loved and get connected to others.

The Fundamental Differences Between Men and Women

Without being influenced with sexual biases, feminist or masculine influences; we can all agree that it is a biological fact that men and women's physical bodies are naturally different. At just a simple visual observation, it can be observed that women tend to hold more body water mass in their bodies; whereas men tend to have more body muscle mass. Speaking on the reproductive end; a woman of child-bearing age sets out to release one and possibly two eggs each month. While men release millions of sperm cells in one *round* of sexual encounter, in which he can choose to have more than one sexual encounter per month.

Taking it a step further in the beginning when a female baby is being formed in her mother's womb, it requires a critical set of genetically predisposed DNA that were passed down from other female ancestors thousands of years ago. This set of genetically predisposed DNA and genes determines specific qualities only a woman can have, personality traits specific for each female and all the things that give her a womanly appearance, to walk and sound like a woman. For women to grow womanly body parts, to get pregnant and carry a child - takes a certain specific set of hormones which are regulated but DNA and chromosomes for a woman to do all she can do to be considered female. These DNA and genetic makeup differences all dictate a woman's emotional and physical traits.

In essence a woman is on the *receiving* end of reproduction, meaning she receives sperm from the mans' penis, which travels through her reproductive tract for reproduction. If this does not happen, reproduction does not take place naturally.

Now on the opposite part of the realm, the exact same goes for a male. When a baby male is being formed and developing in his mother's womb, it also requires a critical set of genetically predisposed genes and DNA that was passed down from other his male ancestors thousands of years ago to give a male his manly genitals, his physical appearance, thoughts and actions.

In essence, the man is on the *giving* end of reproduction, meaning he gives or imparts his reproduction into a woman, is symbolic that the man is on a dominate position. This analogy of differences mentioned is not necessarily a religious or a scientific standpoint but simply a logical and factual analogy of the biological differences in men and women.

The genetic and DNA biological differences I listed are the fundamental basis of how both men and women are different. These differences can heavily dictate how a man and woman operate differently in their interactions together and when trying to build relationships with one another. These differences also manifest itself through how both sexes communicate with one another, how our perceptions and ideas may differ.

To fully understand this dynamic is crucial if you want to attract the love and more important, if you want to maintain your love and life partner.

John Gray wrote in his classic groundbreaking relationship book, *Men Are from Mars, Women Are from Venus*, he notes that a man's sense of self is defined through his ability to achieve results; while a woman's sense of self is defined through her feelings and the quality of her relationships through connections. This translates that men are drawn to getting things done. While women are drawn by connecting to people through conversations and relating to one another.

There is this general common assumption that men may not be as connected to or expressive of their emotions as woman are. This assumption is not accurate. Men are just as emotional as women, maybe even more emotional. The difference is that women wear their emotions on their sleeve – they tend to be more vocal and expressive of her emotions than a man. Whereas men tend to analyze and study, taking notes for a while until they feel safe enough to open up and show his emotions *through his actions*. I further theorize that once the man meets and connect with a woman whom he feels very comfortable with and feels that he can trust; that man will do almost anything for her.

Women and men are both emotional beings. But both express their emotions differently. These fundamental differences that both men and women have, has sometimes made it hard to maintain a relationship and love. For fulfilled relationships, it is imperative for both parties to understand these fundamental differences. Although both women and men have some differences - to the same account it is important to keep in mind that both sexes are of the same human race, so there are way more similarities than there are differences.

Environmental Adaption

Environmental adaption relates to the environment and society that individuals live in and how, over time individuals can change to adjust to fit that environment in order to survive. This adaption is present because of genetic survival instinct we have as humans. As human and living organisms our bodies are equipped to change if need be, in order to survive in a given period; short term and in the long term.

For a metaphoric comparison this would be synonymous to a backup generator used for back up electrical power during power outages. If the electrical power goes out or dysfunctions, the generator automatically kick in and turn on to give energy or electricity. This is the same idea in environmental adaption our bodies are designed to do this.

I would like to take this a step further as an analogy – the cities that occupy the Northeastern Coastal United States, sits closer to sea level, ground level. The Northeastern sea level is lower than the level of the very high sea level that Denver, Colorado sits. Nicknamed the "Mile High City", Denver Colorado's official elevation is exactly 5,280 feet above sea level or one mile.

Both, relocated and native residents, have an increase in the size of their lungs due to this high altitude. Doctors and scientists have scientifically confirmed that after being a resident of Denver their chest and lung size increased to breath better in the high altitude. If this adjustment does not happen there would be a plethora of deaths due to breathing issues. Annually, there are deaths associated to high altitude. On the other hand, some residents actually experience the opposite and develop lung and breathing conditions over time.

Based on the adaptive instinct in our natural human DNA, environmental adaption kicks in to for us to survive for the long term. Once a Denver resident woman gives birth to a child, it is said that the children's lungs are even larger than that of other kids who live in other United States cities with lower altitudes than Denver, Colorado.

This particular dynamic can be compared metaphorically in relation to love and relationships. As humans, our view of love, relationship and how to attain them have changed over the years. How we view each other as different sexes; the role of what a man and a woman contributes to one another; and the expectations of them both have also changed and evolved overtime.

Entropy in Our Society

Entropy is a dynamic in physics that is defined as the more you have in an area, the more chaotic it will become. For example, if there is a drawer in the kitchen, holding one knife, one spoon, and one fork, it is easy to see the spoon, fork and knife in the drawer without any confusion. But at the point that one would add more spoons, knives and forks – that drawer would become more and more unorganized and all over the place.

We can relate this analogy to the human experience and how it relates to how we all may have changed our views of love, life mates and relationships. Overtime our society have become so crowded and loud with our daily lives; it affects how we relate to one another. Families tend to live further away from one another, we work longer hours, we have to keep up with the latest gadget and technology that is released every six months to a year.

In the 1960s and earlier, men were the primary breadwinner in a typical American home, while the woman stayed home and took care of the home and family. There were no cell phones, if you decided to go out to eat; the idea of eating out was considered a treat or a luxury - even going to McDonalds. There were not as many restaurants to even eat out at, because most families prepared their meals and ate.

In the 1970s and the 1980s when I was growing up during that particular time, I remember multiple generational families lived in the same home of the huge brownstones and row houses in the USA Northeastern coast in cities lIke Boston, New York City, Philadelphia, Washington DC, and other cities where the majority of Americans lived on the east coast. It was more of a cooperation with families as they shared responsibilities. Families shared responsibilities like bills, food preparation and cooking, babysitting and household chores. In the typical home you could very well see grandmother and grandfather, with aunts and uncles - intergenerational families living in the same home.

On the entertainment and technology side, the entertainment was paced at a lower speed. An Atari game console would last for about two or three years before a new and improved version was released. At the grocery store to purchase food, there was not as many variations or flavors of the food item as today; there were one or two options to choose from.

Today, we live in an ever changing society world. I refer to it as a "microwave" society, a quick, fast and a hurry society. Our technology is upgraded once every six to twelve months; those huge, three-floor Northeastern brownstone houses have been converted into offices for business and commerce; those food items have expanded to a plethora of different flavors; you can collect a few quarters to eat dinner at McDonalds which has a 90-second maximum serving promise, we work the most hours in a workweek than any other industrialized country; and so on and so forth.

Our society is in a hurry, quick and fast. There is never really enough time.

You may ask me if I feel this is bad changes. These changes in our society are not necessarily bad changes. What is constant is change. Change is inevitable. But women and men are still women and men. DNA does not change. DNA have not morphed our sexes into different sexes...we all remain to be either man and woman, with genitals intact. This fast paced societal environment has cause this physics dynamic of entropy in our society. Sort of like a fast paced society with multiple dynamics causing distractions in how both men and women relate to one another. They When it is all said and done, every change comes some sort of sacrifice. We sacrificed our patience in relationships and love.

Patience as it relates to our lives in love and relationships have been affected. Patience is the number one issue most us have in finding and attracting love. The lack of patience has ravaged and destroyed lives and some people have made bad decisions due to lack of patience. As a society, we've lost our sense of patience in the process of love and also have lost our patience in the process of allowing ourselves to grow, learn and becoming whole in order to attract love and a life partner. It is important to know these foundations in order to make changes in your attempt to find love and to maintain a long term love with your life partner. In the following section we will discuss how to slow down the pace in your own life and allow a calmness that fosters an environment for patience. It takes some practice and time, but with come commitment it can be done.

Self-Care and Self-Preservation

Self-care can be defined as any intentional actions you take to care for your physical, mental and emotional health. Self - preservation can be defined as the healthy self-care actions you take that to preserve yourself in the long term. For example, if someone make a decision that would cause stress in your life, that can affect your self-esteem and outlook in life. This stress can also affect your emotional well-being causing depression or anxiety. While studies have shown that depression and anxiety caused by long term stress can lead to hormonal changes in your physical body, which can then elevate those hormones to unhealthy levels, which can cause weight gain and certain health diseases later on down the line. This health issues will not preserve you in the long term and can cause early unpreventable death.

Disease comes from the root words "dis" and "ease", meaning one's body is not *at ease* with itself. Disease does not always have to be like a serious cancer diagnosis or some other serious physical ailment. It can be emotional burnout, physical or emotional abuse as well. If you had some kind of abuse, self-care and self-preservation is an important part of your healing process. Self-care is unique to each individual. But here is a list of ideas to get you started in developing your own self care plan tailored for yourself. With so much negativity in today's world; this can be an overwhelming battle to take on, but taking it a few steps at a time will help you reach and achieve the goals of self-care which can lead to self-preservation in order to prepare and/or maintain a healthy love and relationship.

Steps to Better Self-Care and Self-Preservation

Eliminate negativity – This goes all across the board; with friends, family, acquaintances and social media. If it does not breath life or positivity into you, maybe you should remove it or take a break from it for some time.

Write down positive affirmations and sayings – Frame them and post them at your work desk; or subscribe to an app or a social media page for daily sayings to be sent to you.

Breathe life into yourself – A few times per week, look into the mirror and love the person you view. Out loud, tell yourself that you are awesome, hot, sexy, amazing, beautiful, handsome, loyal, honest, intelligent, successful an all-around great person. If you pride yourself as a spiritual person, trust that your maker made no mistakes on you. Believe in your faith that your maker is superior than you and is all knowing and believe that you were made the way you were intended to be made by your maker. There is no such thing as a nose that is too big or lips that are too small. Love your eyes, nose, lips, hair, voice, height, weight...just love who you see in that mirror.

Workout and eat well – Studies have shown that working out – even for a little as 10 minutes per day can help alleviate stress. Stress can wreak havoc on your health, your weight and can also age you prematurely. Studies have also shown us that unhealthy foods and in particularly fast foods can cause food addictions and cause many health diseases. Despite your busy schedule, make time to unplug and relax. Prioritize and make time for what's important. Take a short brisk walk during lunch or right after work. Food prep, cook meals ahead of time; buy groceries in advance and cook on your days off to store the food in the refrigerator or freezer throughout the week.

Be still and connect with yourself – Slow down, stop and be still. With such busy schedules and heavy demands in our lives, we have diverted from being one with ourselves and listening to bodies. Take 10 minutes per day turn off your phone, television, close the windows and sit in a quiet area, or outside and breath in the air, listen to the wind; take a bath while reading a magazine; sit in your bathrobe and soak your feet in a nice foot soak.

Laugh and dance – Our jobs and careers have turned us into semi-robots becoming a little too serious than need be. Try to lighten up and not to take your daily life so serious. Laugh, I mean belly laugh!

Connect with your inner youth. For me, watching classic Tom and Jerry episodes help me connect to my inner child, my inner youth. Boy, they make me laugh! Whatever is your laughter preference just do it and enjoy yourself. Nothing is too immature to be silly, just laugh without worrying about acting like an "adult".

Learn when to say no – Being a people pleasure can cause you to overcommit yourself that can cause unnecessary extra stress in your life. Learn when to say no. Be direct and firm. Consider giving another alternative or a compromise. Don't feel guilty. Be honest with yourself and what you are able to do. You are only one person.

Both, self-care and self-preservation are both forms of selfishness. We have been raised to believe that it is not good to be selfish. A healthy selfishness is totally okay and normal. It is crucially important to maintain your good health both physically and emotionally. In order to help someone, you have to first be alive and healthy yourself.

Knowing What You Gotta Do First

To become a physician, one would be required to fulfill the necessary requirements to be licensed to practice medicine. This preparation path ensures adequate education and experience to become successful in the medical field. It entails for the aspiring physician to enroll into a premedical program to complete the introductory courses which set the basic foundation of the medical skills needed for him or her to go onto successfully complete medical school. These specific courses taken include science, anatomy, and others which contain important skills for the student to develop into a well versed medical doctor. Each branch of classes is to also help develop certain personality traits needed to be a successful physician.

Science and mathematics courses are required to help develop and sharpen critical thinking, analytical skills needed to treat patients and diagnose diseases. Anatomy, physiology and health courses are required to understand the basis of human anatomy and disease. And so on and so forth. After successful completion of premedical school; medical school and residency which, is another word for on-the-job training or apprenticeship; is the final step to becoming a doctor and to successfully pass the board examinations. All the above mentioned requirements are for preparation; to prepare and develop a long term and a successful doctor. Even after a license is achieved you would still have to continually maintain that license to practice and work in the field they may be required to complete continuing studies to maintain the license. This required to go back into the classroom and "brush up" on the industry is all in the hopes that the licensed professional will keep abreast of their field and industry and not get lagged behind.

To take this further, this same idea and dynamic works in love and relationships. Once you find that love you desire or your life partner mate, in order to achieve a long term success in love and your relationship; first and foremost, you have to prepare yourself; to allow or attract a healthy love and relationship and lastly, once you find that love and relationship, you want be able to maintain it to last for the long term.

Preparation for love can differ from one individual to the next. Based on your personality, your experiences, your expectations and how much growth you need or how much growth you may not need. But all in all, when it is said and done; if a true healthy relationship is desired, then you have to do what you gotta' do and take the necessary steps needed to get love and keep it. As a pre-medical and medical student is dedicated with his or her studies, their goal to become a successful physician—you have to decide that you are dedicated to do the necessary work. You should be willing to step up to the plate to work on yourself. Working on oneself is a continual thing We all can make adjustments to ourselves, none of us are perfect. If there are tips you can take to improve your love life, start now, one tip at a time!

Tips for Working on Yourself

1. **Work on yourself inside out** – Improve yourself and commit to take the necessary steps needed so you can to work through any old issues that you still may be struggling with that is left over from childhood. These issues can manifest itself as unwanted behaviors or unworkable beliefs that you may have copied from you parents, siblings, family members, peers or any other parental figure in your past. If you need to speak with a professional therapist or counselor to get through some hard issues, it is best that you do so. Seeing a therapist or counselor is the same as getting a medical physical checkup, it is okay to speak to a professional who will be neutral and will listen and also help to analyze your feelings clearly and understand some issues so you can make changes accordingly.

2. Release your secrets – Release those close guarded secrets that you are terrified that someone might find out about you. No one is perfect. Maybe you sweat a lot, or snore, was teased when young about your weight or your height, or maybe you were in an abusive relationship, were hungry a lot, did not grow up in a best environment. We all have had things in our past that we may feel too ashamed to discuss; but its best to let it go, be released. By keeping them close on our chests, each day, those skeletons will eat us up bit by bit. So release them. You don't have to tell anyone but maybe write them down and read them out loud to yourself. Know that it does not define you. If you need to speak to a therapist or counselor, then find a good therapist in your area and go for a couple sessions to speak to someone who is on neutral ground.

3. Reevaluate your relationships with family members and friendships – Positivity breeds positivity. Whether you are single, married or divorced and working on yourself to attract a different kind of partner than you had before, it is a great opportunity to look at the relationships with friends and family members that surround you and to notice who you are attracting in other parts of your life. For family members, sometimes it may be hard to totally avoid seeing some while at family functions and events. Or you feel obligated to be in connection with that family simply because they are family. But a toxic situation is a toxic situation. And it is up to you to decide what to expose yourself to. You may not be able to change that person but you can protect and change yourself. Family counseling is also an option to get through issues with any family members. In your other relationships, like friendships or with a partner, it is up to you to analyze them and make a decision if it is healthy for you to continue. In the same way as love-relationships, not every friend has to be in your life forever. It is always a good time to let go of those toxic relationships to make space for possible relationships that are more nourishing and supportive. Learn when it is time to let go of unhealthy and toxic relationships.

4. **Declutter your home** – Believe it or not but clutter in the home is symbolic to your life and the emotional state you are in. It can include old items you like to hold on to and not let go. It is best to look at each item and decide if you have not used it in the last year, or if it is not a family heirloom, then you may want to donate it to local charity, friend or family member; or toss it out.

5. **Change the way you make decisions** – Analyze how you choose your mates. Many of the limitations that you face in your love-relationship life are often self-imposed. It is due to negative beliefs that you may have about yourself and towards other. I will elaborate on this further topic further in each parts for man and woman.

6. **Have your finances in order** – Finances are a major player in a relationship. If the finances are not in order it can cause a heavy stress and resentment in the relationship. If you have a healthy love and life partner, try everything in your power not to allow your relationship to go sour over finances. In Part three, we will go deeper into finances and how it affects marriage and long term relationships.

Dating Essentials

Now that the foundation of love has been set, it is now time to get into the actual dating side of things. Always remember these two words: anywhere and anytime! This means anywhere and anytime you can meet your true love and life partner. Always keep that in the back of your mind. If you are just divorced, or going through a breakup, or have been single for a while... remembering this will help ease your feelings of frustrations of being alone. You could be in the grocery store, at the car wash, at the gym, in a class, crossing the road, driving down the street, at the library, volunteering, at a concert –anywhere. The possibilities continue, and that is the wonderful beauty of it all, because with fate and at that fateful moment, is because you cannot control it, and it usually comes when you are least expecting of it. Ask anyone who has found their love partner, they can confirm that it all happened when least expected. For me in my love experience, when my husband and I take a look back we can attest to that. So this is why one need to be ready, both sides should be ready. So remember it can happen anyplace and anywhere!

Another tip to remember is that the cards are always shuffling; somewhere someone else has just broken off their relationship or getting ready to break things off, or divorce. Whatever you believe – whether through religion, spirituality or science – whether it is God or luck, when you meet your love, you will know; if not then, but eventually you will know that the timing was perfect and on point. So it's best to work on yourself while your future partner is working on themselves so once your paths cross, it all goes well and it snaps in place like a missing puzzle piece.

Google Investigations

To Google or to not Google? When the dates are fresh and anew, most people get tempted to do some investigations of their partner to see if there is anything suspicious or illegal, lurking. With the internet as a daily tool we use every day, it is easy to view an individual's public records. Many people utilize this method to learn more about their possible life partners. It is definitely a tool to use to gain understanding and insight on someone's background. It is also imperative to remember that sometimes Google will not give us everything we may need to know about a person. Sometimes potential criminals never had a previous record. Because of this, it is important to note that Google may not give us all the answers we are looking for. So just because you may not find something on a person via Google doesn't mean anything. Never solely depend on a Google or a search engine search, also use your gut feeling and look for red flags.

How Long Should You Wait to Have Sex

There is no right amount of time to wait for sex. This is because we are all different people with different situations, experiences and relationships. However, if your desire is for a relationship to flourish and last long term, I say wait a while before being sexually intimate. Instead of setting a wait time, it's best to look at different clue markers to determine if you should have sex. Look at markers like: If you know a lot about the person, his/her friends and family; you have a certain understanding of each other and have discussed different topics about life; you feel that you have a lot in common in values and morals. After a few dates, maybe you would know if you feel comfortable. If you are really looking for me to give you a time mark, I would suggest after a three or four-month mark,(about 12-14 dates) this way, you were able to get a general idea if the dating would flourish into a relationship or may not work. Be sure to make a clear headed and conscious decision on this and not get caught up into the moment to later have regrets.

Health Testing

It is best to take care of your general and sexual health. In this day and age, it is important to put yourself and your health first. Before having sex without condoms be sure to get tested for STDs and HIV together. It is best to go together because you both would be there together to witness the results first hand. Going to a health department in your local area offers free testing. Having a discussion about such topic can be discouraging or fearful. Even a virgin who never had any type of sex would be scared to take STD and HIV tests. It's just the way it is. It is definitely a serious subject. But it must be faced and addressed. If your dating partner seem to never want to discuss the topic or never seem to want to agree to get tested together, then maybe you should seriously reevaluate if you should still continue on with the dating.

Aristotle's Three Kinds of Relationships

To examine the true path to happiness, the Greek philosopher, Aristotle wrote in his book of ethics, his three types of relationships. According to Aristotle - and I agree; two of these types would never work out and one is the particular kind we should all be striving to attain.

1. Relationships of Pleasure – Relationships that are all about the

pleasures of life. Sex, drugs, partying, alcohol - just all about turning up! These relationships cater to the bodily excitement and pleasures, it does nothing to nurture the soul. These physical pleasures will never be enough to sustain a healthy relationship in the long term.

2. Relationships of Utility – Relationships that are all about fulfilling the ego. Having a trophy partner, for gaining status, attention, for looks, power or being in love with someone's potential or what they could be, rather than what they actually are at the moment. This relationship will never be enough as well, because over time it is about ego and it can never bring true happiness to sustain a healthy relationship in the long term.

3. Relationships of Shared Virtue – Relationships that bring out the best in one another. Both partners in this relationship nurture each other's soul and challenge each other to grow into their highest potential. Aristotle considered this the best option when looking for a relationship. It is not as easy to find this kind of relationship. But when you are with someone who inspires you to be better on a daily basis, then you know you have something amazing going on.

What Aristotle was saying is that long term happiness is what relationships of shared virtue offer. The key to this is taking the time to get to know your dating partner on a deeper level versus what's just on the outside. Not because he has big feet, a nice car or handsome looks - or not because she has a big butt or has beautiful facial features. What's also imperative is to take the time to know yourself as well. You cannot offer yourself and time to someone if you don't know what it is that you want as well. Being single is not a bad thing. Singlehood can give you time to spend with yourself and get to know yourself deeper. It is best to know yourself first and handle any lingering issues you may have to be ready for you true love to attract to you. It's not good for you to be so quick to fall in love with any person that comes your way looking good, ready to party or sounds good. Save yourself and preserve your energy for someone who deserves it.

Part One
For Men

Chapter 1
Being a Whole Man

"Be really whole and all things will come to you."
-Lao Tzu

We live in a broken world. A broken world full of broken lives, dreams and promises. Relationships can become broken and hard to deal with. Almost everything around us appears shattered. But in the midst of such - to live a happy life, one can take necessary steps to being a whole man. A whole man is defined as a man reaching his maximum potential of what is life is intended to be for him. You are a king within your own right and is the master of your own destiny. Being a whole man allows a man to make the necessary decisions in order to live a great life without much drama. We as humans will always encounter some sort of drama. Being trustworthy, loving, loyal, helpful, friendly, courteous, kind, brave, courageous, clean, physically strong, mentally awake and upholds moral values. Being a wholesome man, doesn't necessarily mean; how much money or material things you have acquired. It is your internal qualities that you possess. Something that cannot be bought and this is priceless.

In order to attract a healthy love and meet the demands of the relationship, you must be a whole man. While being single and before you embark on a relationship, you should commit to yourself to everything you possibly can do to help elevate your subconscious mind up and clear yourself from any hang-ups or emotional baggage you may have so that you attract a different kind of woman the next time around in your relationship.

If there is a relationship that you want to improve in your family, maybe it's with a parent, brother, sister or any other family member, then now is the time to do so. If you are married or in a healthy relationship and you are finding that you have some long lasting relationship qualms with a family member, now is the time to improve that relationship. You will realize that if you do this, unknowingly it will affect who you attract. Your familial relationships don't have to be perfect but it is better to make peace and work on them. If you work on them it shows your future love that you have the care and drive to evolve in your relationships rather than staying at the same place or focus on upsets from the past.

If you are already in your thirties and you still continue to still blame your father or you mother for not being there the way you needed throughout your childhood, then that could alter how you make choices in a partner. These issues can push away an amazing partner and love. So try to work through any issues you have concerning your family. Focusing on how you are the master of your own destiny regardless of what happened in your past. At some point you would want to take responsibility of your own life choices and behavior. So that you can work through what you need to, let it go and move on. If there are experiences of abuse, then it's best to seek counseling to get through the issues that are bothering you or blocking you from meeting the love and things that maybe affecting you in how you maintain your relationship.

Becoming a Whole Man

1. Surround yourself with great people.

It is crucial for a man to be sure to delegate a positive group of people in his life. Be sure to have positive, strong and accomplished individuals in your circle. Men tend to have less of a support system as compared to women. Therefore, be sure to be surrounded by positive uplifting mature men. If there are some men around who are negative, you may have to distance yourself with them in order to maintain and preserve your positive energy.

2. Dump unworkable relationship beliefs.

Many of the limitations that you face in your quest to finding true love are self-inflicted, because of these negative beliefs you have about yourself. Some belief thoughts are: "I am better off alone" or "Women always want to tie me down" or "Women are crazy". If these statements hit home for you then your unworkable beliefs may be part of what stopping you from finding what you want. If you want to meet an amazing woman, then it is best to have beliefs that empower you and keep you persevering without giving up. If there are issues stemming from the relationship you have with your mother, subconsciously, the way you view and treat your mother, reflect how you view and treat women.

3. Work on a career or trade.

When you set out to embark on a new relationship, the ultimate goal is for it to last for the long term. Having a means to provide or add to the table, is what drives the core of any man. When a man can provide something, he feels happy, fulfilled, he feels like he accomplished the world. Therefore, while you are preparing yourself emotionally for your queen woman, it is a great idea to take up a trade, a class, go back to school and master something that you always wanted to do. If you are already in your career field and is happy with that, then maybe you can pick up a new hobby and try something new and exciting. You can go with family members, your friends, old college buddies and etc.

4. Surround yourself with other happily married couples.

Surrounding yourself with other happily married couples will train your mind and also help you visualize a happy union. It will also help you view healthy marriage as an amazing experience.

5. Change your woman selection skills.

Do you tend to attract the "crazy" women or women who seem to never really care or appreciate all the things you do for her. Maybe you are simply attracting women based on looks or what they have to offer as far as their appearance.

6. Work on becoming a leader.

Sharpening your leadership skills are imperative into a successful you and to ultimately find a healthy love and partner. Women are subconsciously are drawn to men who are natural leaders. It makes them feel protected. Taking initiative in the relationship sometimes will show you are a leader. You can work on your leadership demeanor at work. On the other hand, if you are in a position where you are not able to sharpen your inner leader, then volunteering as a team captain or organizer can help you tap into your leadership side. Quality women love this. A feminine woman love this trait in a man.

7. Breathe life into yourself.

Love yourself inside and out. Each morning and each night before bed, breathe life into yourself. In private, out loud tell yourself that you were placed on this earth to do what you are set out to do and whatever you are placed to set out to do, you will do it in an amazing way. Tell yourself you are great; that you are a king; that you hold inside of you what creates life; that you are not defined by your muscles; you are not defined by your height; you are not defined by the size of your penis; you are not defined by what happened to you in the past. You are an amazing individual and with a man no life can come forth whatsoever. Know that you are worthy of an amazing woman who can support you and your ideas.

Chapter 2
Understanding Your Personal Needs from A Woman

When you are ready to search for the love of your life, it's important to know that everything you want in your heart should reflect your actions. Within the world's population; there are more women than there are men, therefore it's easy for men to get mind-clouded, confused and discombobulated on what his true needs and wants are. When there are many choices, sometimes it can present an issue. It's crucial to be clear and on point in what you need and want from a woman. *There is no such thing as perfection.* Again, there is no such thing as a perfect woman. We have all heard that phrase before but in reality it is very crucial to apply this dynamic to your subconscious. This particular perception has held many men back from attracting, attaining and maintaining a true love and life partner.

Because men have more options to choose from, I feel it is important to tackle your wants and needs. This will help you easily identify a true quality in a woman instead of just *seeing* what you like in a woman and assuming that is what will last. To also limit this common mistake made by men is to take into self-inventory of your actual needs and wants from your future love and life partner. One way to figure it out is to organize what your emotions, needs and wants are, and to write them out to visualize them. On a notepad, write out different qualities you may want in a partner and list ten to fifteen qualities in the order of preference. Once you decide which qualities is best for you,

you should take into account your own qualities and personality and how these two personalities would mesh together. If both of you are good at planning everything, it may be hard to add some spontaneity in the relationship. If both of you like to spend money, there may be some overspending financial issues down the line. If both of you like to tell jokes, it may become quite exhausting overtime. Lastly, write out a relationship and love goal for yourself.

Pick seven top qualities you want in a life partner. Some examples are:

- Kind, sweet, out-spoken, loving, spontaneous, giving, sexy, professional, educated, an employee or an entrepreneur, warm, laid back, driven, shy, sensitive, loyal, independent, quiet, balanced, adventurous, funny, optimistic, organized, a little "hood", classy, happy, introvert or extrovert, realist, idealist, sassy, courageous, gentle, God-fearing, soft-spoken, understand kids -

Once you have picked seven top qualities for both yourself and a mate, write them out and create a clear goal. Be reasonable in listing your goal and time frame (e.g. My goal is to meet a woman that is giving, independent, loyal, introverted, organized, friendly and emotional within two years and to be married within 4 years.) Keep your goal in a safe place and don't be discouraged if you haven't reached your goal within your goal's time frame. Be patient, your future love and the universe around that all has to be in line with you as well.

Beauty vs. Personality

Please keep in mind not to list any appearance qualities in your relationship goal. It is best to list personality qualities. Appearance qualities are superficial qualities; and therefore, can fade or improve over time. For example, a woman who is currently 145lbs. can gain weight in five years; and visa vers, a woman who is currently 320lbs. can lose weight in five years. Whereas, a woman with a pretty face can age overtime, she can attempt to avoid this by receiving facial rejuvenation surgery, Botox, cosmetic surgery, surgery to add fat, cosmetic surgery to remove fat or get liposuction. But overall, the irony of this beauty thing is that it fades or matures, it's not forever - therefore the cosmetic surgeon cannot perform a liposuction or the removal of an uncaring heart or surgically remove dishonesty or a disloyalty out of a woman who lack them. To also add; the cosmetic surgeon in turn, cannot inject or give positive qualities like loyalty through Botox procedures. A doctor cannot inject care, compassion or humility. Physical qualities are all superficial and will not provide long term healthy love and relationships. It is the inner personality qualities are more important than outer appearance.

Chapter 3
Communication Differences

It's no secret that men and women are wired differently and because of this, communicate differently. It is imperative to understand this differential communication so that your expectations of communication are realistic with the opposite sex. This understanding help build to successfully build and maintain a healthy relationship. Women find that talking and relating to other women and sharing their personal feelings, fulfilling. Whereas, men are more actions based, and is fulfilled when he solves an issue or accomplishes a goal. He may feel close to talk about it and express his feelings once he achieved this goal or solved a problem, but in general men are more actions based and they themselves find it hard to comprehend women's communication difference of talking and sharing their emotions as much. Women love to discuss topics that are on their minds to release stress, but men talk about their problems to find a solution. Here is an example:

If my husband and I have a disagreement and his brother called, I began to vent to his brother explaining to him how I was feeling, his brother's reply was "Sorry, Bayyinah, that happened, but I know one thing...he really loves you so much" after his reply, I felt quiet and dumbfounded on the phone. I felt cut off and frustrated that he did not sympathize with my plight or my feelings. In essence he was saying *"Forget what happened because no matter what- at the end of the day he love you and you both will work it out, so lets cut the emotional stuff."* This is male way of approaching communication. The direct solution. Now, on the flip side, once I called my girlfriend to talk discuss and vent to her about the same issue, her response was different. Her reply: "Aww, so sorry; Are you kidding me? I am sorry honey, and you are right to feel that way". In essence, speaking to my girlfriend gave me the space and comfort to actually feel my emotions in order to move on.

This is the point that we see the differences in communications of men and women. There is nothing wrong with either of the two. However, this is where the problem may arise. Sometimes a woman may feel her man is not listening to her and he is ignoring her feelings. At times he may not be listening to her after the first few minutes of talking, but he is in fact listening, but quietly formulating a plan or a solution in his head while you are rambling on with details and emotions. Meanwhile, his partner may continue to go on and on but at some point he has become frustrated, and eventually he withdraws and resort into his shell. His shell consist of – remaining quiet; if he live is a separate place, he may retreat back to his own home to think of the solution in peace. This can be the start of even more serious issues with his woman, who may become more frustrated, and later believe he doesn't care or that he went home to even see or meet up with another person.

In many instances, it isn't the case. It is imperative for women to understand that in conflict to allow her man to retreat and withdraw to figure things out on his own. Give him some time. And likewise, it is important for men to understand and try to listen a little bit more with his partner and love. However, women particularly should further understand that they cannot change a man and turn him into her "*girlfriend*" to make him talk and talk. Women should always have a trusted girlfriend on deck and ready to call up and share her emotions with. And the same goes for men, he should understand that he cannot change a woman who is connected to verbalizing her emotions, and because of this she is trying to create a togetherness and intimacy with you.

As noted before, in John Gray's groundbreaking book; *Men are from Mars and Women are from Venus*, Gray points out that men are motivated and empowered when they feel needed, while women are motivated and empowered when they feel cherished. When a man does not feel needed in his relationship, he may zone out or draw back, and go into his own "shell". Each day he feels this way, the less he has to give the relationship. Until eventually he will lose interest. Whereas, a woman does not feel cherished in a relationship, she then feels responsible and exhausted from giving too much because she is a nurturer. When she feels cared for and respected, she is fulfilled and has more to give as well.

Men, it is ok to open yourself up a bit more by talking to her and actively listening to her, that way she will feel cherished and loved by you. Ultimately, the way to master communication is understanding these fundamental differences and recognizing that both men and women have different needs that one another cannot meet at all times.

Chapter 4
Getting Over Your Fears of Being "Tied Down"

We have all heard the phrase before; 'Men are afraid of commitment' or men have commitment phobias. But at the essence of all fear, is this feeling that something might be lost. So if you are afraid of commitment or commiting to one person, you are afraid of losing options and freedom in different aspects of your life. But here is the catcher: no matter what - every decision we all make in life, means losing other options. No matter what we do, there is always another kind of option of life one could have lived. Now with men who have a commitment fear, fear making the "wrong decision". What I noticed is that the irony of the fear of being tied down is that there is this mask to cover up a strong desire for love, companionship and security a long term healthy relationship only brings. In essence, some men fear what they really want and need most.

You ask where does the fears come from? These fears were developed from rejection and disappointment. Rejection and disappointments in previous relationships or experiences with family, friends, peers or at work/career. Believe it or not work experiences can also affect how one view relationships. Maybe you've experienced a relationship in the past where you felt trapped and suffocated in, and because of this experience, you vowed to never allow yourself to feel such a way again. Maybe you fear the possible future relationship could dissolve or end while you've invested so much into the relationship.

maybe you avoid commitment because you feel the woman may take your assets or money. Maybe you witnessed a rocky, unhealthy relationship with your parents and have your mind set that "no relationship or marriage ever works out". On the flip side of it, maybe you never saw your parents together so you feel that you do not have a "blueprint" to follow to maintain a healthy successful love or marriage. The root at all of the above mentioned dynamics, is unresolved issues. It is important to refer to Chapter One called *How to Be a Whole Man* which tackles on how to release unworkable views that can be a roadblock to meeting that amazing woman.

If prolonged and deep seeded enough, all fears have its own consequences – and this is where the problem lie. In the long term, consequences of your fear of being tied down can lead to the possibility of living a severely lonely life and throwing away a perfectly good life partner and love.

Another point to note and keep in mind is that some commitment phobia men may knowingly get into relationships they know will not work out. This is a coy to cover up their fear. This is a way to run from commitment and it is convenient. Men afraid of commitment may become involved in a relationship that they know deep down inside is not workable. He may also end up dating someone or get involved in an ongoing sexual relationship with a woman of mediocre, easy or weak relationship qualities just to bypass time. All of this and to the fact of knowing that it will not work out. Overtime this sort of behavior can lead to feelings of void and loneliness. If you are a man who is experiencing this or you are not sure if you are, the following four tips can help you identify if you have some commitment fears. Once you release your commitment fears you can then open yourself up to find a healthy love and long term relationship.

Are You Afraid to Settle?

1. Take a long and hard look at your relationship history.

Did you seem to run out on a good and promising relationship? Looking at your relationship history and see if there is a pattern of running off on some seemingly good women and relationships. While reading a magazine recently, I came across an article that read: The One that Got Away, Burt Reynold Misses Sally Field." In the article Burt Reynolds the actor who is 79 years of age at the time of the article. He was quoted saying, 'she was the one that got away...men do a lot of stupid things to mess it up with the perfect woman." When I read this article it I realized, here is this 79-year-old man. You do not want this to be you; looking back on your life after 30 years and still regret allowing the one to get away.

2. Ask yourself what are you really afraid of?

Are you afraid of losing the relationship, your single life, your independence, money, extra sexual options or freedom? After asking yourself what are you particularly afraid of it is important to note that if it is fear of giving up money, independence or freedom? Because no relationship or healthy love would take away all freedoms or independence. In actuality a healthy relationship with a whole woman will help meet your needs in regards to independence and freedom. This relates to Aristotle's Relationship of Shared Virtue (found in the Introduction) theory of being in a relationship of shared virtue – one that inspires you to be great and better each day. If you had experiences in your past relationships with women who were controlling of your life, please note that these were never healthy relationships if it was based on control.

3. Imagine that the fear has gone.

As a society, we are bombarded with the negative points of views. It's all around us, in the new and media. Everywhere. But what if we look at the positives and put the negatives aside. What could be the benefits? What about the marriages and relationships that have lasted and are thriving? We can be so bound up to "all the things that can go wrong" we don't stop to ask ourselves all the things that can go right. There are many benefits to a long term and healthy love. These benefits are both mentally and physically helpful and rewarding, but you've only been focusing on the negatives.

4. Try not to put so much pressure on yourself with the "forever" idea.

Most men with this issue have the biggest fear that in the future the relationship will not work and he have exhausted so much! Remember- Now is all we will ever have. I know it sounds boring and cliché' but we don't know what will actually happen in the future. Life is a series of present moments. You may feel you have all the time in the world but time goes by quickly. So try not to pressure yourself with forever thoughts. Another point is maybe what would work in your relationship now, may not work in the future, then again maybe it will. Life is all about exploration and growth, and meeting that woman who inspires you and welcomes growth and change.

Chapter 5
What do Women Want from Men?

"What a girl wants" is a phrase we hear all the time. What do women actually want? Why are all the good guys single? Do women want a good man? Do she want a man with this or that to ultimately make her happy? What a woman wants can vary from woman to woman based on her personality. But in general a woman's needs go back to beginning of time where she valued from a man connections, security, strength, loyalty, honesty, commitment and sex – yes sex!

Strength – showing assertiveness, being direct, cool and calm is a sign of strength, and women love those signs of strength.

Honesty – Being honest is the building blocks of trust. A woman's desire is to feel safe and honesty provides that feeling for her.

Security – This is figuratively and literally. When a woman who admires you for you, you don't have to be a millionaire. But there are some traits like being ambitious and enterprising that's needed to turn yourself into a millionaire and she would love those traits in her partner. It is symbolic of a man that can get the job done, that is serious, that is strong. A woman wants to feel that you will protect her from physical harm as well. She wants to feel safe, healthy and comfortable. She does not need a man to keep her safe or to bring home all the money. But she in fact like a man to be capable of it.

Commitment and Loyalty – To be cared for and have compassion for is a symbol of not being alone in life. Having loyalty, not running the streets with random woman, being committed to the relationship is what a healthy whole woman wants in her man. Because she is giving you all your needs, she would want those same qualities in her man. A woman wants to know that she is the queen of her man's heart and that no other woman really matches up to her in her partner's eyes.

Sex – Yes, sex. Women love sex, just as much as men. The difference is that women tend to value emotional connections during se, a little more often then men.

Chapter 6
How to Harness Male Self Control

Self-control is defined as the ability to resist urges when it is profitable for you to do so. In essence, it is the strength to put all things into priority and context before acting upon it. Our society is faced with too many options and choices. This is one of the driving factors of why men cheat, and how some men do not desire to settle down. There are simply too many options. Therefore, in order to keep up with your self-control and keep it into context, it is important to know the difference between "preferences and options" and to also make moral decisions and good judgement between these options. Too many choices may hinder quality. Something may be so common that the quality decreases. This is the same idea with having so many options in women.

A common psychology study experiments on self-control are done on children to see their reactions to self-control. A psychologist may sit in a room with marshmallows with four or five-year-old kids. The experimenter will leave the candy or marshmallows on the table and tell the kids, that they can have one marshmallow right now, and, if each can wait fifteen minutes, each can have two marshmallows later. After telling the kids the rules, the experimenter leaves the room. The kids who successfully held off generally do so by distracting themselves with playing, singing and covering their eyes. The children that gave in to the one marshmallow temptations usually did so right after the experimenter left the room. When doing this psychologists try to understand is if children can grasp the idea of deferred gratification— not engaging in something pleasurable now so that one can enjoy more benefits later. Deferred gratification and self-control is closely related.

If self-control or deferred gratification is not practiced and you aimlessly go about your life without self-control, you can cause yourself a domino effect of serious life issues. Let's say he was lonely and became sexually frustrated. Instead of using this sexual energy and harnessing it into a successful business, a hobby, looking for a new job or to connect with a long lost relative connection; he begins to act out on those sexual feelings. In time he may get a woman pregnant that he never intended to get pregnant. After so much anger and resentment from not snagging a relationship with him, she decides to take him to child support, where eventually his license is revoked or is arrested and he is not able to get to work to continue to receive his income. All the self inflicted issues listed were root caused by lack of self-control.

Oftentimes we hear that it is a woman who made the wrong choices in men, they say; *because her father was not in her life.* Barely do we ever hear the men's side of this kind of dynamic. There are a lot of men out here who may have had a disconnected relationship with their mother or father, that a was void of affection or lacked attention as a child. And as an adult he began to act out on those repressed feelings of emotional neglect. Some men, in the end would have a very promiscuous lifestyle with women, or men. This dynamic is seldom addressed because of a double standard that men are sort of expected to be sexually free and promiscuous. But if a woman do it, she has issues. But in reality this goes both ways. If you realized you lacked the attention or affection as a child and this may cause you to be sexually promiscuous, then it is time to address the issues and work this out. This will free you from holding onto such heavy load. Having self-control can preserve you and take you far and beyond in life.

Six Steps to Harness Male Self Control

1. Let go of any past experiences that may be contributing to your commitment fears.
2. Get enough sleep
3. Meditate more
4. Eat healthy foods
5. Manage stress
6. Set your daily goals and stick to it
7. Practice Deferred Gratification - which is the ability to resist temptation for an immediate reward and wait for a later reward. Resisting a smalle but more immediate reward in order to recieve a larger reward later.

Chapter 7
Falling for Mrs. Wrong

Men are hunters by nature and love the thrill of the chase. Most men like Mrs. Wrong because she represents that chase. It is every male's dream to ride in on a chariot to tame or save that bad girl aka Mrs. Wrong. But we all know that this is a fool's goal. As much as a good girl likes a bad guy; a good guy likes a bad girl, for the adrenaline rush. This is the reason men often find themselves dating Mrs. Wrong. Mrs. Wrong is elusive and can never truly be tamed until she is ready to. But this will not stop a man from trying over and over again. He may get burned every time but the thrill of the journey is just an amazing adrenaline rush.

At some point, a man should begin to reach his maturity level and realize it's all about priorities and deciding what he truly want in life. As human beings, we are people of habit and sometimes it is simply hard to break habits that men also love an adrenaline rush. A good quality man desires a woman and to settle down to build a future together. He desire to be with and find a high quality woman who he can trust, who is great sexually, is smart, and can build a family for the future and can also handle the household. Not necessarily a house wife, but a woman who is resourceful, good with money, able to give him advice at the end of a long hard day's work. He may also want that bad girl quality in his wife. This is where the issue comes in. Finding those qualities to balance out both, the excitement and calm in a woman is important. For a healthy long term love, it is not advisable to have one or the other. When you meet the right woman she will possess both those qualities for you to enjoy the duality of both dynamics. Just be sure, she just isn't Mrs. Wrong. Below you will find ten signs that the woman you are dating may be Mrs. Wrong. If they are familiar in the woman you are dating, then it is time to re-evaluate.

1. She lacks a caring heart.

2. She only calls you when she want sex.

3. She has no real friends; she doesn't nurture anyone but herself.

4. She is not close to her family members.

5. She never offers to pay at any date nights after a couple dates.

6. She is unappreciative of your kind gestures.

7. If you have kids from a previous relationship, she doesn't make an effort to connect with them.

8. If she has kids from a previous relationship, she is not involved in their lives as she should.

9. She lacks short-term and long-term goals.

10. She doesn't seem to inspire you or bring out the best in you.

Chapter 8
Preparing to Become a Husband

1. Learn to be faithful
Learn and practice self-control. Most infidelity instances are masks to cover up some other deep rooted issues in the relationship that has not been successfully addressed.   To avoid infidelity you should firs communicate effectively (step 7) and avoid placing yourself in the environment of cheating traps. Never be alone with a potential cheating situation, with someone who you feel sexually or romantically attracted to. Also never confide relationship information with anyone you are attracted to.

2. Master the art of financial strength
Being financially wise as a man, and understanding the dynamics of money, savings and investments will help run your household more smoothly when you become a husband. There are many financial courses and apps to better understand money and finances.

3. Learn to plan and include your significant other in your life
Begin to open up your space in life. Learn to include your woman in your life. Invite her to a family dinner or event. Allow her to hang out with you and your friends. Allow her to be more present in your daily life. Feel free to open up.

4. Be a leader
You can work on your leadership demeanor at work, and if you are in a position where you are not able to sharpen your inner leader, then volunteering as a team captain or organizer can help you tap into your leadership side.

5. Be ready for commitment

Being whole and emotionally healthy will help prepare you for being ready for commitment. Deal with any lingering issues from previous relationships or family issues.

6. Master the art of understanding women

There are some things you may never fully comprehend in regards to a woman. But the key is to understand that there are fundamental differences in how a woman view the world around her; her desires, needs, how she view her man, how she communicate. It is important to constantly work on being patient and understanding the fundamental differences of both sexes.

7. Learn cooperation and communication

Cooperation can be defined as the process of working together to the end. Cooperating, trust, compromising and communication is the foundation of a strong marriage union. I further discuss communication in the Introduction and in Part 3.

Part 2
For Women

Chapter 9
Being a Whole Woman

"I am a divine original, fashioned by God to be radiantly beautiful."
~Unknown

Many women have not quite reached their full potential and evolved into the women they are destined to be. Not to confuse this with perfection. As no one will ever reach a perfection state. But what I mean is that the goal is to release and bring to life whatever qualities and strengths you were blessed with. Once your strengths and qualities are fully identified, developed and released, it will radiate from the inside out through your appearance, your demeanor, and your attitude. In the end this will naturally attract a healthy love. Because men are great at non-verbal communications, a great man with great intentions will approach you when least expecting.

The bottom theme of this is that whatever aura you give off is what you radiate or draw to yourself. If you have anger, resentment and drama in your life it radiates through your face and body language. This would attract men who prefers women with low self-esteem, drama, anger issues. The man's conscious would say "Oh she looks like someone that I can easily manipulate" – Let me get at her. Most likely he would not even think to approach a woman who looks happy, easy going and strong minded. On the other hand, if you have happiness, positivity and strength in your life it radiates through your body language as well. This would attract men who value a happy, drama free, confident and easy going woman. He would subconsciously say to himself "Oh she looks like someone that can light up my life and I can build something with." – She looks amazing. No woman will attract a healthy love if she is not whole and have not quite recognized and embraced her full potential. Please heal emotionally before you embark on a new relationship. The below are steps to become a whole woman.

1. The Power of Releasing Resentment and to Forgive

Mahatma Gandhi said, "The weak can never forgive. Forgiveness is the attribute of the strong." Personally speaking of my own experience, I had to let go of resentment from past experiences. In actuality, we all have held on to these feelings before. Unless a person is a sociopath – who is rarely with feelings, once someone hurt you the feeling of anger or continual anger which is resentment, lingers. When we hurt someone else we feel remorseful and would generally address this and apologize. In regards to receiving an apology from someone who offended you, keep in mind that it may not happen. Some people may have an ego, denials and/or embarrassment holding them back from apologizing. Remember, this is not your issue, it's their issue. Therefore, sometimes we may not receive that apology that we want or we may feel we need in order to move on. In the case you haven't received an apology or an acknowledgement of wrong doing, we still have to find the strength to move on. One of the major ways to help with the forgiving dynamic is not to think about the past or that bad thing that has happened.

Release it. Know that time heals all wounds and the time to let it go and be free from it is now. Maybe you received an apology but you still can't seem to shake it off. No matter how many therapists or counselors you see, it still is up to you to decide in your mind to release that resentment and anger.

2. Concentrate, Meditate or Pray

It is important to go into your own quiet space, once per day to meditate, relax and release. Stay calm for at least 20 minutes per day. Whatever your faith is or outlook in life, it doesn't matter, but it is safe to say that every woman need some time to herself to calm down be serene, and focus.

3. Delegate a Committee of Positive Individuals

Reanalyze your personal relationships, and weed out any negative or toxic people. I am not saying to call them up and say they are not good people and therefore, never call or contact you again, but what I am saying is that maybe you should begin to space yourself away from those relationships and ultimately part ways. A litmus test to decide if your friendships are toxic, is to see how you feel after you speak to them or is around them. If you feel happy and fulfilled after the connection, that's great, but if you feel drained or as if you should always be on egg shells, then maybe the friendship relationship is unhealthy. Obviously, if you have a friend who is going through a trying time, they may not be themselves for a spell. But with an ongoing connection that is uncomfortable, then it may be time to part ways. This can also be attributed to family relationships as well.

4. Build Your Self Esteem

We were put on earth for a reason and it is important to know that it is not by chance or by accident. It was destiny that you are here on earth. Know your value, embrace yourself. Build yourself up daily and designate a "no media day" once or twice a week. Where you commit to no live television, internet, social media, and/or no news - try avoid reading and watching and listening to anything negative in media or even to watch anything negative. Maybe watch inspiring "chick flicks", do a puzzle, play a board game, call up a family or friend to have an old fashion phone conversation, or do an exercise DVD and enjoy yourself. This would help restore your faith in humanity, in people.

5. Learn to Say No

People pleasers can find it hard to say no. Maybe this dynamic is rooted in being rejected or denied or even to get attention, but ultimately learning to say no will help prevent burnout from over committing yourself. This burnout can lead to unnecessary stress in your life. Learn how to say no in nice ways like:

a. *"That won't work for me right now, but I will let you know if anything changes."*

b. *"Sorry, but I can't today."*

c. *"I really appreciate you thinking of me, but I just have too much on my plate at the moment."*

Be mindful of persuasion techniques like reciprocity, which is a form of manipulation. This means they will give you something before asking for the favor. Don't be fooled into this trap.

6. Help Others

Doing things for others is not only good for them and a good thing to do, it also makes us happier and healthier. Giving connects us to other people while, building stronger communities and societies for a better world for us all. So if you want to feel good, do good! Make it a priority to do for others whether it is small, unplanned acts of kindness or regular ongoing volunteering it is a powerful tool to boost your own happiness. You can help your family, friends, strangers, co-workers, young or old, local or international. Remember that giving isn't all about money. Giving a kind word to someone on the street in passing, a smile, time, care, skills or attention. A lot of times these gifts mean as much if not more, than monetary gifts.

7. Make Peace with Previous Romantic Relationships

A poet by the name of Pablo Neruda wrote "Let us forget with generosity the people who cannot love us." Some people simply lack the ability to love in a healthy way. And to take Neruda's advice; to wish them well on their own journey. If someone lack the ability to love, it's not your job to change that.

Letting go of a past relationship is like mourning a death. Releasing that relationship and letting it go will help you. I personally had to call up an ex-boyfriend to politely inquire about what actually happened between the two of us and why he did the things he did while we were together and towards the end of the relationship. I expected a negative feedback and reply, but to my surprise we spoke as adults and he was able to give me insight into the dynamics of his life while we were together. After that conversation took place, I felt so much better and was finally able to put the relationship questions to rest after the years. It later helped me and how I related to my husband, and in turn, it helped my marriage.

Realizing that sometimes this may not be an ideal option for everyone. If you decide to contact an ex, do so with out any remorse and with and open heart and understand you have to be prepared for it to go either way, negative or positive, but it's an option. Another option is to write your feelings down on paper as if you were talking to your ex. Then place the letter in an envelope as if you were going to send it to your ex in the mail. But do not send it. The idea is to release your feelings you harbored inside. You also understand that you will have to simply let it go and any questions will go unanswered. It is up to you to release this in order to make peace within yourself.

8. Learn to Smile More

Smiling can make you happier and more whole. Making an emotional face or suppressing a smile can influence your actual feelings. There are studies that prove that even forcing a smile genuinely decreases stress. A feminine smile is one of the fundamental steps in attracting a man. A lot of times just a smile alone can attract a high quality whole man. I further discuss femininity more in chapter 11 entitled, "The Feminine Woman".

Chapter 10
Allowing Love to Find You

Love is a strong feeling and most people are looking for love. Women are drawn to love. As natural nurturers, and givers of life it's as if *love* and women are closely related. Women are especially susceptible to feeling the need of love, affection, and to find love. Neediness and desperation of some women often times is evident through their actions during their vulnerability state while being opened to finding love. The only issue with neediness and desperation is that this will manifests itself in your demeanor, and this demeanor will not be very attractive to a high quality whole man.

You ever noticed, why does it seem so easy for people to find a partner when they aren't looking? It is always the carefree single person who is not looking for love. If you follow these point below, you would not wonder if you should go up to or approach a man. The man will approach you!

How to Allow Love to Find You

1. Finding love should not be a burden or stressful.
Allowing love to happen naturally is your best way to ensure love to attract and find you. When you stop *looking*, the right person seems to walk in the door unexpectedly. It will come naturally.

2. Patience will bring the right person along your way.
More than likely, when you are desperately on the lookout for love, you

will be more susceptible to fall for any man that comes along. Patience is the key.

3. Laws of Attraction.

The law of attraction states that "like attracts like" - not that you want someone just like you, but what you want is for a healthy love to attract itself to you. Being positive, confident and relaxed will most likely attract a healthy love to you when the time is right.

4. Allowing yourself to be opened and ready to receive love.

Love is like a spiritual connection, a magnetic force. The right man or mate will naturally be drawn to a woman who is opened to receive love. She can be completely covered up in cloths, without showing her "assets", that right man can look into the eyes of a woman and know. When a woman carry herself with grace this is in the sense that you co-exist with yourself as a woman with love and caring. Most relationship advice books offer readers relationship advice based on spiritual aspects or a psychological aspect. My goal is to give you relationship advice from a totally different point of view with a combination of the above mentioned viewpoints intertwined.

Close Your Legs if You Want Closure!

Why, oh why do we sometimes fall into the trap of sleeping with exs? Thanks to a culture that is more accepting of casual sex, breaking up and still continuing the sex with your ex is something that people do often. But is it a wise decision? No, if you broke things off with an ex, it is best to respect the boundaries of the breakup and move on expeditiously. Sex with no strings attached is a misconception, and meaningless sex with your ex is also a misconception. Have you ever heard someone say, "Wow that sex really healed me!" after having sex with their ex. No, it doesn't happen.

Yes, at times you may be lonely or feel you need sex. But in reality you don't. The more you lay down and have sex with your ex, the more you build an unhealthy connection and attachment with your ex. Remember, you (or your ex) broke things up for a reason, and now it's time to just move on to the healing level from the issues that may begin to stem from the relationship. Small and/or major issues. You do not want to continue on with an unhealthy relationship.

What you choose to tolerate will constantly happen over-and-over again. Your ex may begin to take you less serious over time. Give your ex a hug, wish him well on his way and be on your way as well, because when it's all said and done, in the end you would want to make the best decision for your emotional health without carrying too much baggage. Do not aspire to be a bag lady carrying around all those baggage's. That's not a good look. But aspire to be a woman with an empty luggage ready to meet a high quality man, to end up traveling together!

Chapter 11
Being a Feminine Woman

"A woman who embraces her femininity is a woman who embraces her power."
~ Kelly Mcnelis

A feminine woman is a powerful thing! A rarity- she does not consist of just a "beat" face, nicely done hair, nails, the latest fashion or shoes. It is the highest beautification of mankind. It prides itself in her ability to love, her spirituality, her radiance, her delicacy, sensitivity, creativity, charm, graciousness, gentleness dignity and her quiet strength. This manifests itself differently in each woman. But each woman possess it. Femininity is a woman's inner beauty. A woman's inner beauty is what a man will fall in love with. This is the key to any man's heart. It is like a magnetic force to men. It has nothing to do with being a plus size woman, or a slender woman. It has nothing to do with her height or her breast and derriere size. After a few dates, maybe you haven't been getting those return follow-up calls back from him. I am going to show you how he will not hesitate in calling back! When a man sees a feminine woman, he is looking at her class, tenderness and virtue, he will naturally want to be more of a gentleman around her, to naturally treat her with the ultimate respect. Every man on planet earth is wired a certain way that triggers his responses to love and attraction. And a feminine woman is what attracts him.

What is femininity? It is the natural essence of what a woman is.

In our society today, women live a very masculine life. They work a masculine job, speak in a masculine voice, act and uphold themselves as if they are competing with other men. By no means am I saying this is not right. It is the destiny to achieve success and reach the goals we all set ourselves to do. It does not mean you have to give up your career or jobs, it just means that you cannot always live in the masculine mode all the time. To attract a healthy love you have to leave the masculine mode at work, and it's imperative to learn to achieve a balance between femininity andthe masculine mentality of getting results done at work.

It is important to know that being in constant masculine energy will kill the attraction that most men would feel for a woman. Why is this? Because he would just see you as one of his boys, and there is no male-female polarity or feeling. Sometime he may like to watch sports with his woman, or have a conversation, but this is not all the time. For a man to feel connected to you he must feel a feminine side. Therefore, most of us women who have careers, jobs must understand in order to be a feminine force, we need to come back to that feminine core and spirit. Most women reject their femininity because most of us are confused. Research shows that we are being consumed with tens of thousands of sales messages and opinions per day. So this causes us to become confused at what we need to do as women, and how to conduct ourselves as feminine women. This is also how a lot of us women have lost our female intuition that we are all inherited with.

How to Attract Any Man with Femininity

Any woman can attract a loser, but it takes a lot more to attract a good man. Most men who are good quality men, have more options in women, simply because they are good men. However, good men desire a woman who can bring something to the table as a woman; to make him feel like the man he is. Men are connected to their egos by nature, therefore being a woman that make him feel alive and respected is what men desire from a woman. It is like a matching missing puzzle piece. Being a true feminine woman will attract any man of great quality. Practice these four tips to be the ultimate feminine woman to naturally attract an amazing partner and a healthy love.

1. Feel Yourself

Go into a place alone to cry, scream and I mean wail if you need to. Whatever has hurt you over the years, feel that, feel vulnerable, connect to your physical pain and emotions that allow you to feel yourself. As women, we have gotten away from feeling anything as a woman. We have become afraid to be a woman, So it is vital to emotionally and physically detox ourselves through crying. This help stops us from being the robot women we have become. Outword evidences is you get sick, the female genitals tighten up, you lose your sex drive, you can't be yourself and you hold resentment and anger in your body the organs that gives women their womanly looks. You smile becomes tight and fake, your face is no longer radiant, even some women outright begin to miss periods or go into early menopause in their 20s and 30s. Feel yourself, feel your experiences, feel your pain. This is the first step to opening up your feminine side.

2. Sing and Dance

Every day before you start your day, turn on some positive music and just sing and dance in an unplanned way, feel your female organs, roll your hips, your body. Feel the music and just dance. Connect to your feminine side.

3. Take Care of Small Details

Get pedicures, manicures, facials and massages.

4. Carry yourself in a feminine manner

Walk, gracefully with a straight posture, without dragging your feet; smile and make feminine eye contact- those eyes of innocence

5. Learn to Keep Your Masculinity at Work

Keep your results driven personae at the workplace and know that once you leave work, you have to reconnect with your feminine side. Maybe on your way home from work you tune into on some light instrumental music in the car or on your headphones while on the bus or train. This will help you release your masculine energy. It can also help release the work stress from the day. You can also think of those things that help you connect to your feminine side, whatever that may be. Work on this everyday and soon, eventually it becomes second nature.

Chapter 12
Stop Running Those Red Lights!

Each of us are equipped with an instinct. It's sometimes referred to as the fight or flight response. It is a survival skill that humans have been wired with for thousands of years, when faced with danger or stress, the brain triggers a signal and tells the human to stay and fight or get the heck out of there – flight. Human instincts are rarely ever wrong and we all should work on connecting with our instincts and acting on them more.

It is best to use our instincts to **prevent** hurt, harm or danger in our personal lives and love lives, instead of playing damage control later on while in danger or in trouble. My mother always told us as kids "It's easier to get into trouble, but it harder to get out of trouble." When red flags arise; some of us choose to acknowledge them and avoid the person, while some of us choose do the total opposite- ignore them and stay. Some people are afraid to face red flags; or may feel they are overacting and if they address the issue they may offend the person. Avoiding red flags can cause serious problems and can be disastrous down the line.

The problem is not that the red flags exist (you can not change that), it is a matter of changing the actions you take once you actually see them. If you do not change how you react – flight or run after you see red flags; then you're always going to get the same exact results over and over again. This is because you will always ignore the red flags by lying to yourself and saying it's just your imagination or you want to give the person the benefit of the doubt. Below are a list of the eleven common red flags most people ignore. If they are familiar, please work on this area.

Common Red Flags to Stop Ignoring

1. He withheld information from you.

How many kids he has; if he did time in prison; he never seem to want to discuss information about his family life; but you told him so much about your life and in detail. This withholding information is to hide something from you. Do not continuously ask or inquire for information if he or she does not want to give it up. Simply see this as a red flag. It is up to you to continue or move on.

2. He is getting too comfortable too soon.

Sometimes some people just "click" well, but in general bonds take time to build and need to be nurtured, so guess what? He doesn't love you just after just two weeks of knowing you. He has other motives.

3. Always want something from you.

You receive a random text, "I miss you", followed by a string of favors – can I have this or can you do that. All relationships are based on a give and take, but if you find yourself always giving to the person, then it's time to walk away before you get your emotions deeply invested and then it would be harder to walk away.

4. They Make Suggestions as to How to Look Better or Make Your Life Better.

Maybe it may come off as being caring and helpful at first, but in the beginning giving advice so soon can be a sign that he actually wants to control you. You have been you for years and if you are happy with who you are, he should be as well since you just began dating.

5. Your Friends and Family Don't Like Him and He Doesn't Like Your Friends and Family Too.

If you have true friends, they love you and want the best for you. If one friend says something, then that's one story; but if you are constantly hearing complaints from more than one person, then it's time to seriously reanalyze him. On the other hand if he just don't seem to like your family and friends, and question all your relations with them, then he is trying to isolate you so you will not have a support system to call him out for any wrong doings he may do to you in the future.

Chapter 13

How to Change Your Man Selection Habits

Do you find yourself often wondering, "Why do I always pick the wrong men?" or "Why do I always pick the same man with a different name?" Your man selection skills and habits are actually connected and related to your heartache and pain. It's a reflection of your inner self. It's also a familiarity of your comfort zone. There is a subconscious or a hidden part of us that draws us closer to particular people who trigger a comforting or a familiar feeling. This is how we all make connections and form friendships. But when a woman's man selection skills is off; she pick the same kind of man each time and will eventually get heartache and pain. When a woman has unhealthy man selection skills, she thinks that when she meet a man she has a connection with him and she feel those feelings of chemistry and fireworks. But actually, what is happening is that her adrenaline is rushing and her inner drama queen is having a blast. Maybe in her mind in her previous relationship, she became "bored" with that good quality man, and in turn is craving for excitement and attention from the opposite.

If this sounds familiar, identify this and commit to changing your man selection skills. If you do not change your unhealthy man selection habits, you will always find yourself drawn to the same kind of man, and his name is *Heartache*. The key to attracting or allowing healthy love to find you, is to discover this dynamic and make the necessary changes as soon as possible. Once you make changes to this subconscious action, you will see that the men you meet will change as well.

Steps to Changing Your Man Selection Habits

Whitley Gilbert: I would like a man who is educated, enterprising and ambitious
Dwayne Wayne: So you wouldn't mind if he was poor?
Whitley: That type of man is never poor.
~A Different World

1. Break the cycle of bad selection skills.

Look at your past relationships and determine the common reoccurring theme and figure out where these patterns have their roots. Identify these roots and also identify your desires and your fears of being with a good man or partner. Face these fears and address them head on.

2. Speak life to your inner self .

Work with yourself and your subconscious mind, maybe you have self-esteem issues stemming from your past via childhood or previous relationships. Speak life into yourself, build yourself up, refer to the Introduction section of How to Work on Yourself for further readings in this book on this topic. If you seem to need help with this, try go to a therapy for a session or few.

3. Place value on his character.

Placing value on a man's superficial qualities – e.g. his sexiness, his money, his big dick, his car; will always leave you in danger where you may find yourself with a man who is rude, angry, have excessive baggage, disloyal, non-communicative and hurtful. Rather than the superficial qualities, place high value on his character – his soul, one who is honest, empathic, caring, communicative, someone who values growth. Take the time to get to know a man's personality and qualities.

4. Run if You Come Across Red Flags

If you identify red flags, simply run. You do not know the source of his pain or his story. It is just best to avoid such men. You will save yourself so much disappointment, heartache and pain in the future.

Chapter 14
Ms. Superwoman – The Single Mom

Being a mother takes strength, patience and so many other qualities to raise and nurture children. She tirelessly works inside and outside the home to make sure the children and the family is well taken care of. It takes a mighty someone with great diligence to raise her children into adulthood all alone. It is much easier to run a household for women who have a partner to help her. But with single mothers it takes extra skill and diligence to complete double the work of caring for the children, being the bread winner; and finally caring and nurturing herself. This is the single mother. It is estimated that single mothers make up close to half of the U.S. family structure population. According to many social indicator studies show that if the trends continue, in the U.S. it is estimated that in the next 20 years most homes will be occupied by single parents in particularly single mothers.

Single mothers give love to their children but many single mothers never fully love or receive that love reciprocated until later on in life. As babies are held, hugged and yearn for mothers affection to love and cuddle them. As the child grow up into teenage and adult years they no longer want or allow their mothers affection as much, because they no longer see themselves as a baby and desire to be free and independent. In the meantime in her most lonely nights alone as a woman she desires a romantic affection herself. It is a natural feeling. It is important for single mothers to use their support system of family and friends for help, and also to relax and release the stresses of being a single mother. It is her duty to work on being a whole woman (Chapter 9) and to practice self-care and self-preservation (Introduction). If she does not practice and work on these dynamics, she becomes frustrated, unworthy, impatient, lonely and oftentimes, as a result will become one of the prime target profiles for the master manipulator. Be aware of the master manipulators! Do not fall into the trap of these men.

To help avoid this - stay active, build a group of single mothers alliance group – rotate baby sitting on weekends, go out on a date; allow other single mothers to go out on a date. Plan outings or sleepovers with the children. Take the children out to volunteer activities for less fortunate children. Examples include visiting orphans and orphanages with kids who may not have any parents. Ultimately, understand your children is your only return on investment – no man who have not given you a healthy love or commitment. Do not trade that.

Chapter 15

Mrs. Independent

You can do it all. Actually, you are more than capable to do it all. You are successful; you went to an institution of higher learning and copped your degrees; worked hard in your respectful career and you feel you are just coasting enjoying the benefits that you reaped from your hard work. No one can take your accomplishments from you. No one can take away your education. You come from a line of strong women, or maybe you had no one to guide you while young, but still was able to rise above enormous odds.

When your car breaks down, you know where to go for the best service. If anything needs fixing around the house, you can handle that to. You have an amazing career, great friends and family, you travel and participate in the activities you enjoy. But in your quiet moments, you often wonder what your life will be like with a love partner in the picture. You often tell yourself "Just be happy with yourself" or "I am married to Jesus" and "The man will come along when least expect it". That's very true, but the most important step is that maybe you aren't taking the necessary actions or making moves to open up yourself to attract a healthy love and life partner.

If you are looking to meet someone amazing and to date, you may not make it happen tomorrow, but your actions and adjustments now can up the odds it will happen sooner than later. You have to be willing to commit yourself to put in the work to make it happen.

How Independence May Be Sabotaging Your Love Life

As John Gray, Ph.D. mentioned in his book *Men are from Mars Women are from Venus*; men want to be loved differently than women do. Whereas women long to feel adored and secure, when men tend to crave the feeling of being needed and appreciated for what he can do or bring to the table. Men have to know that they add value to your life and that their presence makes things better. This is what drives a man, deep within him. This very dynamic can be applied not only to single women but with all women, married and single. This is a dynamic to consistently practice and go back to and remind yourself of, even for those who have been in a marriage or in a relationship for years. And that is to allow a man to feel like he brings something to you.

Historically, men have been the providers and they are wired this way, so they have to know that they are still bringing something to the table even in this day and age. If you have the *bases* covered, that actually can be intimidating to a man because he will feel that he has nothing to offer you. This has nothing to do with him and being confident as a man. It is just how men are. They need to feel that they are bringing something to the table. There is nothing wrong with being successful and driven and an all-around awesome woman who does it all! However, keep in mind that there is a difference between an attitude that gives off *"I've made a good life for myself"* and one that screams *"I don't need a man!"*. I am in no way suggesting that you should cut your hours at work or get rid of some things you own for a man to provide that, but that idea is simply about opening up and allowing a man and love into your life.

Ways to Open Up Your Heart

1. Don't try to do it all – It is okay to allow someone into your life by helping with things around the house. It's good not to be a burden on others and learned how to handle business on your own. The problem is, overtime you may be making things harder on yourself. You maybe allowing more stress that can lead to mental fatigue, when these things are not as necessary as they seem. Take it easy, on yourself. Allow someone to do something for you. And don't worry if they can't do it as good as you. Sometimes you may be surprised.

2. Keep giving respect – Sometimes when doing things on your own often, you are not as easily impressed. If a man does something for you be sure to respect and appreciate it, no matter how small you may think it is. Men show how they feel through actions, so if it is for you that is his way of showing you how much he loves and/or cares for you. Give respect. Breathe life into your love. Appreciate his thoughts, his kind gestures. No matter how small or large it may be.

3. Keep an open mind, be humble – Being successful is all great and is to be commended. But what if your company folded, or you were laid off and is suddenly unemployed? It is always imperative to stay grounded and humble because we all are just a few paychecks from being in a certain financial state or unemployed.

Chapter 16
Mrs. Fix It, Ph.D.

"My name is Jane Doe, and I think I can fix men. It's true. Behind my loving, giving and educated self, I've completely fallen for the Mrs. Fix It trope that glorifies the idea of me, the woman acting as the ultimate fixer-upper. He is kind, sweet, giving, love my kids, love me, is dear, sexy, has amazing oral and vaginal sex skills. Yes, he has serious anger issues. But I can fix that. Yes, he cannot seem to keep his job. But I can fix that. Yes, he asks for money a lot. But I can fix that. Yes, he can be a little jealous. But I can fix that. Yes, he gets into trouble. But I can fix that. I can fix it all – to the point where he depends on me, and only me, for all his weaknesses. In time, eventually, relying on me to save him from himself. I happily oblige until the life is being sucked out of me and I begin to grudgingly regret it."

Sincerely,

Mrs. Fix It Ph.D.

So many women are fixers. Attracting the same type of men – men who need to be fixed. These include men who are cheating men, drug dealing "dough boys", commitment-phobic men, alcoholics, drug users, emotionally damaged men, sociopaths and narcissists. It is like you are a magnet for such types of men- men whose life pieces are scattered all over the place. Some women feel compelled to put these pieces back together. But please note: YOU WILL FAIL EVERY SINGLE TIME. I promise you.

As a giving, selfless, loving woman, you may think you can be that woman- the one who will change him by picking up his pieces. This is the selfless woman. Some selfless women believe that they can change a habitual cheater into a loyal boyfriend. She believes she can get rid of his emotional baggage he has been carrying around for such a long time. She thinks she can help him walk away from drug abuse or alcohol abuse or get him over his commitment issues stemming from his rough childhood- to work on a stable future together.

Mrs. Fix It attract these kinds of men, because she believes they need her. She feels to end the relationship, would be cold, mean or selfish. She is holding onto that strong desire that it will change no matter how hard it is. She constantly reminds her inner self that no other man is perfect, this is the best she can get – so therefore she has to make it right because she believes she may never get another man.

The problem with Mrs. Fix It, is that she constantly blame herself if he doesn't change. Anytime he fails her, she blames herself. She begins to feel somehow she failed him. The hold he has on her becomes stronger and he will keep the woman around knowing he have nothing to offer her.

The analogy I would like to use to have clarity on this particular dynamic – it is like paddling a boat while being stuck on a rock, the boat is not moving or going anywhere, and with all the paddling; you become tired. The question I ask is: why do you feel the need to help someone else get back in the water?

Women were blessed with a keen sense of inner nurturing, devotion, intuition and care. Women were equipped with this tool since the beginning of time. Women nurture their children, families, friends and strangers in their lifetimes. Women feel others pain, and always want to make sure everything is okay, that everyone is happy. That is a woman. However, overtime it is imperative for Mrs. Fix It to acknowledge the reality is that she is attracting men who need to be fixed because it means that- only through these men that can reveal the reality that Mrs. Fix It may have some issues of her own and she will eventually tire herself from this cycle. There is an urgent need for Mrs. Fix-It to begin looking after herself and nurturing herself. The time is now to realize that a man's happiness is not your responsibility. He is responsible for his own happiness.

You are deserving of a man who don't need fixing up. One who is complete, of course, no one is perfect. Once you realize you are not responsible for a man's issues, you will begin to walk past his scattered broken pieces. It is okay to be selfish. Sometimes you have to look in the mirror and tell yourself: "Stop worrying about other people's misery". Bring the focus back to you and attract the man you deserve. Knowing that it's hard to break habits, but breaking this habit will save you from a lot of heartache and pain in the future. This entire dynamic points back to the Self-Care and Self-Preservation sections in the Introduction. Instead of saving men, you would be saving yourself.

Chapter 17
Understanding Men

Never think like a man. Instead, think like a woman who understands men! Your body does what your brain tells it to do. Therefore, if you think like a man, you will eventually act like a man. There is no way around this. It is best to think like a woman who really understand the foundation of men. Whatever your brain tells you, so you are. Have you ever heard someone say "Think like a child but act like an adult?" No, because it's almost impossible. The brain does what you think and tell it to do. Think like a woman while still being able to understand a man. In essence what men want from women are simple – it is someone to appreciate him for he may do and bring to his partner and family; he want a woman to love him for him; not to be his mother; have fun with him and being easy going. Sex is important and it is often over mentioned when it comes to men. Most men love sex but sometimes they actually enjoy intimate connections, just relaxing with a woman he feels a connection with. In the beginning there are so many sexual sparks and it slows down.

In the classic American movie Rocky 2, the main characters Rocky and his love, Adrian get married. On their wedding night while Rocky is bringing her home for a honeymoon moment, he places her on the bed and says "You are the best thing that come into my life," she reply with a question; "You'll never get tired of me?" and Rocky replies "You aint never getting rid of me," That moment in the movie is such a great moment in love, and the writers put that in the script for a reason. What Adrian asked her new husband, reflects the fear of many women in newly marriages and relationships; is that over time, her husband or man may get tired of her. Maybe afraid that her youth will fade, and he may no longer find her attractive. But connecting to your femininity and being a whole woman will take you far and make any woman keep her girlish and youthful quality that lasts a lifetime.

On the other hand, what if I told you that men have sort of the same fears? As men grow mature they have the same concerns and fears about keeping their youth as much as women do. A man's desire is to successfully provide to his woman and family, being able to make and keep her happy. This also means happy in the bedroom. As men age, so does his hormones and sex drive. As testosterone slows down, his penis may not get as hard, and sometimes with decreased testosterone his penis may even decrease slightly in size. Therefore, as much as women may worry about keeping a man's attention by not losing her beauty, gaining weight or keeping the vagina wet and tight – so does a man is who is worrying about his own. It goes both ways.

In general men want femininity to compliment his masculinity. Simply put, if a man wants a woman, he wants a woman not a woman who acts one his friends- maybe sometimes he like to hang out with his girl! Good quality men like to work hard. When he comes home from a long day's work he would just want to relax. He would not want to deal with an angry wife/partner house chores, over excited children running around and cooking. He need and want someone to ease his day from the hustle and bustle – the rat race. He wants to see his beautiful woman to welcome him home with a beautiful cheery smile and a good meal. Additionally, he need something only a feminine woman can give him – a joyful happy lightness and that innocence of being feminine, this energy soothes a man and melts his heart and make him feel refreshed to ready to take on the next day.

Men Are Visual Beings

Women must know this and understand this. We have all heard our female friends and peers in our society complain or even broken up over their man looking at another woman. They complain and say its disrespectful and they should never do this, they should only have eyes for their one and only. But the truth is - men are visual beings. Once again, this takes us back to history where men looked and sized up a woman's physical traits and assets as a method of determining that she can bare healthy children for him. It does not matter how often or how long a man prays, he will look at another woman. It does not matter how much his wife or partner screams and argues with him, he will eventually look at another woman. That's just a man. They are visual beings.

To fully come to terms with this and to fully understand this dynamic is freeing. To have this understanding will allow you to expect this to happen, and can feel comfortable and not irate or feel you are lacking something. Know that it has *nothing* to do with you, whatsoever. In no way am I suggesting a men watch party looking to vigorously watch women and for them to use their historical predispositions as an excuse to look at women in front of their spouses or life partners. But what I know is that most men always mention that once their significant others "catch" them looking at another woman they get into a huge argument for something minute because many times he may not have even realize they did it, and they had no intentions of ever hooking up, let alone talk to the woman they were looking at.

Now back to women selecting a mature, whole man. A mature whole man will be very careful in who he connects with and who he gets close to. He knows the risks involved and the consequences of losing his love or life partner if he acted on his wandering eyes, thoughts or physical feelings. In no way am I stating that a mature, whole man is mistake proof. He is definitely human, and is capable of making a mistake. But what I am saying is that as women sometimes we can put way too much emphasis on this dynamic. When simply he is just acting out of nature. This is normal. If he claims to be a heterosexual this is what you should definitely expect...at least occasionally. If he is looking at other women in extreme levels, then it is time to sit down and discuss this with him and how he should be mindful that it may hurt you in some ways or can bring you feelings of inadequacy.

What Men Usually Look For

A mature, whole man is not so shallow as you think. He may enjoy the view upon first sight, what they see at first sight but he takes notes on whether the woman is fit for a long term relationship. He immediately put her inside a box. Easy and fun or Long term wife material. On the other hand, we cannot change the fact that men use visual cues to decide a "*possible*" love or partner. A feminist can debate this dynamic but a feminist cannot change the weather; no one can change nature.

According to studies, what men look for in the short term and the long term are both different. They prefer looks in the beginning, but overtime in the long term, they value personality, great hygiene (smell good) and a woman adorning themselves over actual body build looks. Not all men feel the above way, its just a general study. However, keep in mind that men like to know that his woman takes pride and care in herself and her appearance. No matter your religious background men, would like to feel his woman adorn herself for him, even if its behind closed doors, sexually.

Do Men Really Only Want Sex?

Men are frustrated with women because they seem to never want sex. Women are frustrated with men because they seem to always want sex. As human beings, we are driven to want sex through testosterone hormone, which is predominantly a male hormone. A normal healthy man's body produces way more testosterone than what a woman produces. In other words, a man feels the same way after one day without sex as a female feels after twenty days without sex. Knowing this simple difference, you should understand the pain men go through. It is not their fault – they are simply wired this way. Their genetic hormonal make up drives this. Beside for reproducing, sex is a physical act that eases the testosterone build up pressure he experiences constantly. Yes, men can make love to a woman while having sex. But there is a fundamental difference and more to this matter, but in the sake of this section, this explains why it always seem to appear as if men really only want sex. He is driven by sex for a woman he is attracted to, but it takes an amazingly understanding and feminine woman to keep a man and gain his heart, attention and love. In conclusion, No---men do not only want sex. If may appear that way, but it is more complex.

When He Loves His Mother

A man's relationship with his mother can tell you a lot about how he handles women. How a man handles and love his mother is a reflection of the type of bond he would have with his love. I was often told by my mother to always watch how a man treats his mother and the women in his family, as a key factor in determining how he will behave in a relationships with me. In general, men who grew up close to their mothers nurturing them, generally tend to be more sensitive and attentive in his future relationships with his love and partner. These men respect their mothers a great deal because they were raised by those amazing women who instilled values and morals in them. Some morals can include showing them how to value a woman; which includes discipline and self-control; and having a sense of genuine respect for women in general. On the other hand, it is important to note that in extreme cases to this side is when mom dukes may interfere in her son's relationship, which can cause a strain in the relationship. This issue can be dealt with once the son communicate with his mother to slow down a little and to respect his relationship and space.

Now on the flip side of the "momma's boy", there are three other types of men who aren't as close to their mothers. These men can be a little more complicated. Type one is the men who may not be that close to their mothers, but still love and respect their mothers in high regard. They will show their love and relationship respect and love, but they may be a little standoffish, cold and may not be as affectionate as the men who are close to their mothers. With some relationship nurturing this can be worked on and improved.

And lastly here are the other two. These are the men you should see as red flagged so run and/or walk away fast! They have strained relationships with their mother. They are men who have no relationship with their mothers whatsoever, or went through different periods in their life with their mom not being around, and had an unhealthy relationship with his mother. These two profiles of men are the ones that fear commitment the most. They also tend to sleep around with multiple women a lot; they have abandonment issues; are so afraid of commitment where they actually find ways to push a good woman away before catching feelings, attachments or deep emotions. They have not exercised the aspect of fully opening up their heart to a woman. However, it is not your job to mend, mold or change this man or try to help him overcome this deep rooted issue. Women have done enough of this and it has not worked out well for most, as they have ended up with broken hearts.

It is important to note that not all men who have had these mother to son relationship dynamics are like this but it happens more than less. So keep that in mind while dating and while on your quest to attain a healthy love. Take notes on how he speaks of and about his mother, no matter how much or less she was in his life. If the relationship was not as strong, he still shouldn't downgrade or speak negative of his own mother. If he does, this will give you insight on how me may treat and regard you. The man who loves his mother (or grandmother who may have raised him) is the best men to consider when looking for a healthy long lasting love. No matter the "annoying" issues of the mother prying in the relationship, wouldn't you rather have a prying mother, than a disrespectful man? The tradeoff would be definitely worth it.

Chapter 18
The Masters of Manipulation

According to Merriam-Webster dictionary, manipulation can be defined as the act of undue influence through mental distortion and emotional exploitation, with the intention to seize power, control, benefits and/or privileges at the victim's expense. A master manipulator's main goal is to distort your mind, exploit your emotions- with the goal to have the *advantage* to receive something from you. Victims of manipulators experience a repeated never ending cycle of fear, obligation and guilt. The victim is made to feel afraid to *cross* or upset the manipulator, then feels obligated to comply with the request of his or her favor, and lastly feels quilt not to do what is requested. Most manipulators look for their victims who possess qualities like kind hearts, giving spirits and a warm-loving soul. Manipulators are charismatic, charming, intelligent and are simply con artists. They appear as extremely confident, but it's a delusion, in reality they have super low self esteem and confidence, but project the opposite on their victims. This manipulation intelligence was probably gained while on the streets; while being incarcerated or they can very well be an educated professional.

It is very important to understand the difference between a healthy social influence from manipulation. "You scratch my back, and I'll scratch your back" This saying is an example of social influence and the reciprocity idea of *give and take*. It is a principle found in every culture. Richard Leackey, the famous anthropologist that studied the origins of humans said that the reciprocity is an essential human trait that helps us keep the idea of sharing and cooperation with one another. Social interaction happens with most people in generally healthy relationships. It includes the give and take of all relationships. On the flip side- manipulation is like "I scratch your back, but you should scratch my back *and* massage it for about 60- 90 minutes, wax it *and* kiss it." With manipulation, the tradeoff will *always* be that you are giving more than what you receive from the manipulator.

How Manipulators Operate

Manipulators number one holy grail is to first understand their victim. They are sweet, nice and calm in order to gain your trust to open up. They come off as one of the trustworthiest, nicest and coolest people you could ever meet. Once you open up, they understand your weaknesses and your strengths. They take mental notes and store them in their long term memory for later. Once it's time to use their tactics to get what they want- what their victims will experience is almost like a never ending continuous circle of craziness and drama. If you try to cut them off they will never back down easily. It is very important to read through the conning game of a manipulator and be able to distinguish the difference healthy social influence from manipulation. You will find a list below the eight trickeries of manipulators to be successful. Learn these tricks and protect yourself from master manipulators.

1. Study

A manipulator's holy grail is to first study his possible victim. He or she will be nice, gentle and easy going and be a great listener. They will ask simple questions and would appear as a gentle friend who listens – maybe for hours on end to understand you and he or she often will appear as non-judgmental. This is done to establish your behaviors, wants and needs. All of it is a part of a hidden agenda. This particular main dynamic is established in the beginning because this is how the individual understands what makes you happy, sad or angry - your strengths, vulnerabilities and weaknesses. Manipulators prefer people who may have the following personality traits: clean hearted, honest, giving, compassionate, easy going, naïve, genuine. Some personality profiles they prefer are single mothers, independent women and/or single women who just got out of an unhealthy relationship. Keep in mind manipulators can be women as well, they are not just men! They can manipulate men who have giving, kind and genuine hearts.

2. Constant Criticizing You to Make You Feel Low About Yourself

When being constantly criticized it eventually drags you down to the point where you feel totally bad about yourself and second guess yourself and your amazing qualities to take a toll on your self esteem, until you pick back up and do something for the manipulative person then all is well again. You would experience a roller coaster of highs and lows.

5. As Time Progress Verbal Abuse Progress

Once you have opened your heart and shared with him or her your intimate secrets, fears and desires, the manipulator will use this information and constantly bring it up and "throw it in your face" to make you feel bad about yourself. Although you felt you were sharing your inner thoughts and feelings, the manipulators try to make you feel bad about it. They constantly hit below the belt to insult you. Some manipulators may compare you negatively to someone else or create imaginary friends that cosign on their analogy of you, saying things like, "Everyone has said this about you" or "Even this person or that person thinks this way about you", or "He or she said this about you too."

6. Nothing is Ever Good Enough

Some manipulators will always make their victims feel that whatever you are doing is just never enough, this is to continue the benefits. This never-ending ongoing continuous feeling will never stop. No matter what you do, no matter how much or great you do, it will never seem to be enough or make this person happy. You may feel you are stepping out of your normal personality to go far and beyond to make the manipulator happy. The manipulator will continue requesting unreasonable requests. The goal is to keep the manipulation going and going. This will cause the victim to feel drained and always inadequate within themselves. This is a power tactic, to continue the power. And once the victim asks the manipulator what has he or she done for them, the manipulator will always do something for you. But this is so small and minute, it is like crumbs compared to all you have done or given the manipulator. The manipulator will often exaggerate what he or she has done for the victim. The manipulator will use guilt by saying something like, "After all I have done for you". Throwing these things up in the victims face, constantly reminding them that they have "gone far and beyond" for the victim.

7. Rarely Discuss their Past Life in Detail

To discuss their past is just too painful for themselves, therefore manipulators rarely discuss their past in life. Also note, to discuss their past life means you are more likely to see their true person and see their vulnerabilities. Their power of manipulation lies in knowing your vulnerabilities without you knowing theirs. Therefore, they can control the thoughts of their victim in order to receive what they want. If inquired about their life, some manipulators may say things like: "I had to be become independent on my own, or "I had to be a man at a young age, nothing came easy".

8. Great at Non-Verbal Communication

Manipulators are very good at analyzing body languages to decide a person's personality. Within the first few minutes of meeting you, they can read if someone is shy, aggressive and a no nonsense kind of person. They steer clear from the later, the no-nonsense kind of person. This person is someone they despise, and they may forbid you to talk and discourage you to continue the relationship. This strong minded no-

nonsense person can be a long-time friend, a family member or an associate. They may advice you something is not right and to stay clear and away from them. The manipulator may in turn paint a picture that the person is jealous of your relationship. They may make it appear as if the family, friend or peer is trying to turn you against the manipulator and break them up. They may also point out and exaggerate the loved one's weaknesses or imperfections as a way to "turn you against them" and ignoring to their loving advice or to never speak with them again.

Many manipulators are individuals who may have deep rooted issues stemming back to their childhood. Serious abuse probably took place in the person's life and as a result they may be dealing with some mental illnesses. Mental illnesses like; narcissism, sociopath, borderline personality disorder, bi-polar, co-dependency and also drug addictions, and this includes being addicted to prescription medication and marijuana.

Manipulation is a seriously growing trend in our societies worldwide. This manipulation is the cause of a plethora of relationship issues and in extreme cases, the cause of domestic violence crimes, violent crimes and deaths related to love and relationships. Even after a manipulative relationship is over, many victims of manipulators experience some lasting emotional effects from manipulation from the unhealthy relationship.

It is best to stay totally clear away from a manipulator because the ending results may not be good. It can cost you your own emotional health, your freedom or even your life. Some of us may use slight manipulation, maybe to get a ride from a coworker or maybe a wife may suck her husband's penis to get a nice dinner date or that jewelry or dress she wanted. Maybe a husband may be nice to his wife to get that sensual and freaky sex from his wife/partner. However, the use of fear, obligation and guilt is the distinction in a classic tell-all sign of the manipulator. Be wise and be strong. Learn to say no and move on. Learn to love yourself enough to protect yourself. The best way to avoid a manipulator is to NEVER GIVE THEM THE CHANCE! Once manipulations signs are noticed, it just best to leave the person alone.

Chapter 19
The Man with a Wrap Sheet

This chapter is not to paint a bad picture to any of men who have been incarcerated or jailed. Many great men were in fact incarcerated and jailed in their lives – for example men like; Martin Luther King Jr., Malcolm X, Nelson Mandela, even protesters expressing their right to protest exercising their first amendment rights. Therefore, a lot of people who have not committed heinous crimes have been arrested. It is also important to note that there are also a growing number of accounts of people who have been exonerated or wrongfully jailed, proven through the foundational evidence of DNA. There have been numerous records of innocent men being arrested, or some men were given heavy sentences for simple and minor crimes. So this is not an attack on anyone who has been incarcerated.

This chapter is to help women understand their dating pool and what is out there that can hinder or delay your chances at a healthy love. The United States criminal system is the largest in the world. It is said by many, that the U.S. criminal system has the highest incarceration rate than any other country in the world with people of color being more likely to be incarcerated more than whites, with the same offense. Even for smaller offenses, it is proven that men of color/non-whites are more likely to get heavier or lengthy convictions than white offenders. So for a typical minor offense, a man of color would be sentenced with a felony conviction and so on and so forth. With incarcerations rates more than men in college, and according to Justice Department, while extraordinary numbers of men incarcerated, this leave a smaller dating pool of available men for women. Once the men who are available are low, this dynamic may cause some women to go for a male who may have been recently released from jail or incarceration.

In 1971, Stanford University conducted an experiment called the Stanford Prison Experiment (SPE) and it was to study the mental effects of being a prisoner and being a prison guard. It was funded by the U.S. military. Random men were selected, and the plan was to stay in a mock jail institution for four weeks. It only lasted for and concluded after six days. In conclusions what happened and what they found were astonishing on how the different dynamic of jail affects the mind of individuals. The jail environment wreaked havoc on the minds of these men. Their actions and demeanor had changed. Therefore, it is common knowledge that being incarcerated for some time does have lasting effects on one's behavior.

In the 1940s and 1950s there was a theory called bibliotherapy which was developed by Herman Spector, he argued that inmates could be cured through reading. This idea welcomed libraries in prisons. This was heavily and accepted throughout the 1960s and 1970s. This dynamic flourished and became a method of self-empowerment for inmates. Inmates began to be empowered by reading different materials while in jail.

A great percentage of men during this time admitted themselves that they learned how to read and became men because they went to jail and was able to clearly think and read. Something that they probably would not have done while not in prison. This is the incarceration era that gave birth to the evolved Malcom Little to Malcolm X. He, among so many other Black American men, became empowered through being incarcerated and came home to the communities which they lived and tried to impart a wisdom to their families and friends. This was the time that the Nation of Islam, Five Percenters, Black Israelites and other different religious political movements were on the rise. Jails and incarceration gave birth to this "black male enlightenment era". Upon being released, men would often return to their neighborhoods, start their own businesses as entrepreneurs, and took care of themselves and their families.

Current day, the jail environment is not the same. Over time since the 1970s, there has been a change in attitude toward bibliotherapy and therefore libraries in prisons have been removed. In 2006, the Supreme court ruled that denying inmates – who are in solitary confinement, access to books did not violate their constitutional rights. So with a jail system that does not support intellectuality or bibiliotherapy, this causes chaotic environments in the jails. Fights, revolts, killings, raping among so many other things happens very often in today's jails. In July 2015, President Barack Obama addressed male rapes in jail and how he will try to work with Congress to pass laws to protect inmates from the violence. After such an environment, it is logical to know that being incarcerated in today's jail can have lingering effects on one's emotional, mental and psychological state. To help foster transitioning from jail-home these programs and support systems have been removed and no longer funded by the governmment. With inmates leaving jail with nothing to go to, not even a place to say. Being literally dumped into the neighborhoods where they used to live. When someone is living in an environment where they are being served breakfast, being served lunch, and being served dinner and later sleep, this becomes ingrained in his or her actions, one may take on this sort of lazy mentality. I have to note, that not all men who leave prison will take on this mentality. Men who have a firm foundation with an amazing support system from their family and friends are able to maintain a healthy masculine mentality and leave jail to transition well back on the outside.

There is a growing number of women who date men who have recently left jail. This sometimes present issues within the relationship that some women overlook. Once a man has completed his sentence, there is barely any adequate resources for him to take advantage of to help him transition from prison back to regular civilian life. Often, employers overlook and pass previous offenders, as well as housing opportunities. Often, by the time the male is released, his family is overburdened with their own lives; they shun or are not in a position to help. This leave the male with a previous record in a desperate situation. So what does he do? Instead of looking to commit another crime to head back to prison, many begin to look for a woman to help him meet these needs. How do you convince a woman to do so much so soon? Through sex, emotions, sweet talking and through manipulation.

There is a growing number of women dating men with previous convictions. A lot of times the men are master manipulators, verbalizing all he can to win the heart of a vulnerable woman. He can spot and detect a vulnerable woman, from a strong woman. A vulnerable woman may be someone who is a single mom struggling to care for her children. These women are vulnerable because with a workload of working day in and day out to provide, she takes so much to meet the needs of the kids. Many single mothers do not get the help that is needed, so she is on her own juggling. Barely does she get compliments as kids are not at the age to do so at that time. So a master manipulator attracts her and tells her all she desire and wants to hear. His words appear so genuine, true, dear and sweet. This is because he has understood that he has to appear genuine or else she can figure the plan out and not give him the green light. They are generally not his true feelings towards her. It is a manipulation move. He can move in, sell her a total dream, but over time she realized he can never seem to ever deliver in on anything. He cannot deliver because he lacks the required skills and work experience to get a job.

Another woman that may fit the mode of this kind or man; is single, successful women. These two kinds of women single mom and single independent women desire companionship. They may be at their last thread of patience in meeting someone in their lives. Single independent woman may have all the degrees and education, but she is still a woman who desire the comfort and attention of a man. Because he is frustrated with life, the sex is generally good. Sex is the driving force that makes a man do anything. All great men of genius and power used their sex drive as fuel. They turn their sexual energy and aggression into productivity or money. He uses sex as a way to keep the woman's mind blinded by what is really going on. A woman see sex more on an emotional level and is attached to sex and sexual pleasures. It is always best to avoid such individuals, because in recent times there are an increase of men with previous incarceration records who have imposed this mental issues on the woman and her children, raping and killing children. It is best to avoid this kind of person from the early beginning. This will be more easy for you to part ways easily, the longer you stay connected to such man you increase your chances of being stalked without being stalked or just best to because it can become dangerous to your life if you try to leave.

Ways to Identify if He Has a History of Being in Prison

1. He never discusses his past. If he doesn't have much to tell you about it, it's because maybe he is hiding it or want to forget his past and trauma he may have experienced.

2. He appears to have an extensive knowledge on law and criminal laws without being an attorney. If he appears to be an attorney or the DA without having a degree in law or any formal experience, then he is a criminal with a law-judicial system understanding. Meaning, he understands the law through experience and dealing with his attorneys and/or public defenders.

3. His family does not help him or seem to be close to him much. If you meet his family and they appear to not want to have much to do with him, it's because they are happy you are taking his burden out of their life. You ask, how can people be selfish and never tell me their nephew or son or brother can bring nothing but heartache? Well that is how people operate. It is self-preservation. They would rather self-preserve themselves without their family member bringing them extra stress, so they would not give you, "Heads up girl". It is up to you to look out for yourself and do what is best for you.

4. He always seem to want to spend the night at your place and never seem to want to go home. This is because he doesn't have anywhere to go. And if he does have a place to go, he is not fully welcomed there. So he would rather be there with you.

5. He looks for you to cook food for him daily. You should not feel as if you have a son in him. Although we all have to eat and a way to a man's heart is through his stomach, but understand cooking for someone comes from love. It is nurturing, that there is a thin line between giving something to a man who deserves you love and not your love.

6. He asks for money in the early days of dating. Asking for money in the early days of dating is a serious red flag that he is not working and may begin to place all his burdens on you in the future. A whole man will hold a sense of pride or embarrassment to ask for money from a woman in the beginning.

7. Not in his own children's life but seems to seem to want to be a father to your kids. Some single mothers may become blinded by this because they desire for their children to have a father figure in their lives. But this is a serious red flag. How can he possibly love your children more than his own? It is all a part of the manipulation tactic, since he knows your children are dear to your heart and to be close to what's important to your heart, means he is close to your heart as well... to continue his manipulations.

Chapter 20
How to Make Him Propose to You Without You Giving Ultimatums

When your relationship hits a speed bump, and you've become fed up with some of the issues in your relationship. Maybe you have been dating for a couple years with no talks of marriage. Maybe he doesn't include you in his life as he used to by going off with his friends and doing his own things. You feel the chemistry just isn't the same anymore. In the beginning the relationship was like magic, like heaven...but recently things seem to slow down drastically. But the golden rule is to know that, in the end it is wise not to give a man an ultimatum for marriage. Ultimatums are just like holding someone at gunpoint to rob them for their cash. If never intend to use the gun by shooting them, and if they do not give you the cash, what do you do? Walk away without the cash and still be friends? No. It would appear as weak and you could also get into deeper trouble by attempting a robbery. So ultimatums are sort of the same way. If you give an ultimatum and your partner declines, then overtime this may make your partner feel that he or she needs to rush into marriage without allowing the connection to organically grow on its own. And sometimes, ultimatums can backfire. If you give an ultimatum an inch too soon, just as the man is ready and preparing to propose. He may have been out looking for a ring or discussing the idea with his friends or family. So if an ultimatum is given during this time, it most likely will discourage your partner in moving forward with his proposal altogether. Therefore, ultimately, ultimatums leave a bad taste in the mouth of the partner and it can cause resentment in the relationship.

There are four reasons to why you may have found yourself in this situation in the first place. First, it is important to know how most men view marriage these days. In marriages today, men simply do not see anything beneficial in it for themselves. Marriage has become such an unhappy dynamic for so many men, they are so afraid to get married. When single men look around them, they often realize it may not be the best position to be in for themselves. They often ask "what do men really get from marriage?" The images on TV does not nurture or foster great marriage images. Maybe their peers have some sort of marital stress as well. Therefore, many single men just view marriage as a bad investment with no returns on their investments. The secret is to never allow your man, even a good quality man, to feel this way. There are many pretty ladies out there. However, to desire a wife... a man has to feel that if the relationship were to ever end, he would find it *really hard* to find the same kind of woman that he has found what she represent – that whatever she brings to the table it is a rarity to find in today's society.

To further explain how men feel - its that the good quality men work hard. Men may often feel that once they get married, its great in the beginning, the kids will come, once the children are there- it is great to have a family, to feel fulfilled. Then he will work tirelessly to support the family. The wife oftentimes become very busy with work, the children and soon the husband often times begin to feel left out, ignored and neglected. By the time the children are grown, and out of the house there is an empty nest; he feels it's kind of too late, as if he lost the home and his youth in his prime. This is how men often feel in regards to getting married. It is up to the woman to help him feel that he will receive something in the marriage. Something that will actually fulfill his needs as a man and more. The needs of a man can be further read of in Chapter 17.

The second reason you found yourself giving an marriage ultimatum to marriage is that you've made it too easy for your boyfriend. If your ultimate goal is to be married, it is important to have established that from the beginning. It's important to conduct and present yourself as a girlfriend with wife qualities, without giving him too much. Do not treat your boyfriend as if he is your husband. There are even some couples that refer to themselves as husband and wife, and are in fact not married. Do not use these words playfully if you intend to ever be married. Try not to ever live together before marriage; not to share all your finances with one another; do not fulfill all the sexual fantasies he ask of you and the list goes on. A man has to yearn that it's currently great and also gets better with marriage. While in the relationship, if you never drew the line between what he can get while in a relationship and what he can get while in a marriage; then he will always feel he doesn't need to get married. There is no growth room, no limits. Some men even say, marriage is nothing but a peice paper, and therefore, there is no need to get married. It is not just a piece of paper. If you share your time and effort, with someone as if you are married, then both parties should be able to profess and proclaim the love to make it official legally. Also, in dire situations a girlfriend would not be legally considered next of kin. It would be his blood family member(s).

I advise that if you find yourself in a never ending relationship situation, begin to slow down the things you are doing and ween your boyfriend off of all the benefits he receive from you and vice versa, try to ween yourself from him as well. He will never take you serious if you make things too easy.

The third reason you may feel the need to give a marriage ultimatum, is that maybe he just isn't interested in being married. In this situation, you should have been able to pick up the signs of this since the beginning of your relationship. However, maybe you failed to use good judgement and communication, failing to discuss each other's relationship expectations. "We are just taking it easy to see where it goes" or "Right now I want to take things slow" or "I want to know you better before we discuss that" Statements like these are sometimes male communication games. If this is his kind of communication that takes place in the beginning, ask for future explanation; if he intends to be married. Try to see if he has a past relationship pattern of jumping from relationship to relationship. Know that if there is smoke there is fire. You are not crazy; it is your intuition. Most women feel they need proof to see if he has another woman or if he is hiding his true intentions. Sometimes the proof is your intuition and women have to start trusting in their intuition and believing that it is enough.

Patience is the forth reason. Maybe he is simply not ready. Or maybe he never had intentions to be married. Or maybe you are pushing him to propose before he is as ready to get married as much as you are. Lacking patience before a man is genuinely considering marriage to you could mean that you could be missing out on your chance or prized opportunity to get married. Learn more about him and his values to strengthen your relationship by talking about your relationships future without a threat. Plus, don't you want him to propose because he want to – and not because you made him? Never pull out a gun to scare your boyfriend in order to get a ring. When it's all said and done, if you are willing to walk away, then the ultimatum may not even be necessary at that point. If the situation is unworkable and nonnegotiable that you can't be with him under any circumstances, then it's just probably time to move on and allow a healthy love to find you, one who have the same relationship goals, morals and values as you.

Chapter 21
10 Steps in Preparing to Become a Wife

1. Get over any family issues or emotional issues
Getting over any lingering issues that can push your love away will take you far when you get married. If you have to enlist the help of a therapist, it's best to do that.

2. Master the art of trust
Trust issues can be a strain once you are married. Trust issues can stem from previous bad relationships and can be a root of low self-esteem issues as well. Learn to trust. Remember, life itself is a risk!

3. Develop your spiritual side
Whether you are spiritual or not, develop your spiritual side or practicing relaxation and meditation techniques can help you stay calm, relax and to connect with yourself to have an inner peace.

4. Develop the ability to take care of a home
Let's face it, no man wants a woman who lack in the home economics area. Likewise, if your tire went flat, how many women would change it? You would like your man to be handy around the home, so you should also have abilities to keep your home tidy and cleaned.

5. Learn how to cook
The way to a man's heart is through his stomach. I am not saying you have to be Patti Labelle or Paula Deen in the kitchen, but it helps to

be able to whip up a meal for your family. It is also cost effective to cook meals at home saving your family money. If you are not good around the kitchen you can take advantage of cookbooks, cooking apps and how-to videos that are at your fingertips to show you how to cook any and everything. Even how to boil the perfect hotdog! So there is really no excuse to lack cooking skills.

6. Develop responsible money and financial habits

Men love to see a woman good with money. It makes them feel that their queen can handle the castle when he is away or not able to do so. Handling the finances in a healthy and responsible way can make your future marriage and relationship go far. With finances being a major blunder causing divorce and breakups, it is imperative to be financially wise. Learn how give good money saving advice and tips to your future husband. Men love that as well. They feel you are not trying to spend all the hard earned money.

7. Learn how to share and open your heart

We have all been hurt before, bad breakups, infidelity, you name it. But at some point there comes a time to step up to the plate, take that risk and decide to take a chance at love again. To fully receive love, means one should be willing to open themselves to share or give love. Men love to see a woman who has a gentle and possess a nurturing side.

8. Learn the art of compromise

Learn and prepare yourself to compromise in a fair way without sacrificing on one side. Knowing that in a healthy compromise, both partners should give up something in order to compromise in a fair and balanced way. The key is to both feel valued, respected and fulfilled.

9. Develop or deepen your feminine side

Men are naturally drawn to the very essence of what a woman is: femininity. Femininity is the ability to speak gently to him, and not like being his mother, the ability to encourage him, the ability to show him that you respect and adore him. In essence is to be vulnerable. Femininity is something that every woman inherently has, but through our society, has been washed away with our overworking schedules and a busy life. Women who connect to their feminine side are like magnetic forces to men. Learn how to deepen your feminine side in Chapter 10.

10. Develop pray (or develop) for discernment

Praying for discernment or connecting to your inherent intuition is very crucial in finding and attracting a healthy love. Discernment is another word for instinct, but with discernment, it is a more of a spiritual connection. It is the ability to see through game and also recognize honesty and genuineness. There are some individuals that are extremely good at deceit, no one can see the deceitful signs or red flags. This is someone who can be defined as a sociopath – but with discernment, it would allow you to pick up on this if you feel it. Remember, you do not have to have proove that the person is telling the truth or lying - it is just an urging feeling you feel. While dating, developing this quality can protect you from the wrong person or it can lead you to the right person. In a marriage, the power of discernment will help you in how you deal with your husband and with your children in many areas of their lives as well.

Part 3
Maintaining Lasting Love
For Men and Women

" Now that we found love what are we gonna do with it? "
~Heavy D

Chapter 22
Money and Marriage

It is no secret that finances can put a humongous stress on a relationship. They say money and love can be the two ingredients for a divorce. According to Divorce Financial Analysis (2015), finances is the number three common reason for divorce. But in reality this doesn't have to be the case. To maintain a healthy marriage it is important to understand the fundamental dynamics of currency and how money matters and influences the relationship before you even start. It is the foundation of understanding money.

Our currency is simply referred to as "fiat money." Fiat money is a piece of paper that is printed and legalized by the government to buy things with. Other than the fact that the government legalized this, it is simply just a piece of paper. Historically, most currencies in the world were backed by precious metals. To be exact, the United States dollar currency was backed by gold blocks, which was called the "Gold Standard." This "Gold Standard" says that whatever paper money was printed and used, it is backed or can be converted to gold. This meant you could take your money to a bank and exchange it for gold. These gold blocks sat in backrooms called "reserves" at the US Federal Reserve Bank in New York where they still sit to this day. In 1971, President Richard Nixon shocked the world and cancelled this dollar to gold backing. Currently the dollar is backed by nothing, this is what fiat money is. Simply paper money.

To understand this further, let's take a money order. You go to Western Union and give them $500 to purchase a money order. They print this piece of paper stating that it is worth $500. The $500 cash is sitting in Western Union's cash "reserves" waiting to deposit those funds into the account of whomever cashes the money order. The money order would be the US dollar and the cash you gave would be the gold.

At the end of it all, it is important to say that fiat money is simply a printed paper in order to recieve goods and services. Money is important. But simply said, money is a piece of paper (affected by other economic influences) and it is important to see money for what it is.

Tips to Prevent Money from Destroying Your Love

The first step is that you should change how you view money. Point to remember: Everyone is born broke. All children have no money. I say this to even a baby born into a rich family. A baby born into a rich family doesn't have any money, it's their parent's money. Not their own. Yes, the child will grow up with all the amenities and comforts of money and luxuries that money can bring along with possible business opportunities and business connections in the future; but those finances belong to the parents. It belong to the parents until they officially decide to inherit it or pass it down to their child. Even with this situation at hand, the money is still not the child's automatically. In general, before money is set to be passed down to another, before it is inherited- there is a certain set criteria that a person has to meet. The heir must be of legal age and of sound mind which determines if that they are able to receive the money or assets. There may even be other criteria set up by the family member who is passing down the assets or money.

To take this further to use of an example of a "rich" family that we may all be familiar with in our political and popular culture. This is not in any way supporting him, but if we look at Donald Trump and his children. As he was campaigning, he often mentioned his experience as a father and compared his fatherhood experience to his other "rich" friend's fatherhood experience. He often compared how both sets of children were born into huge possible financial and business opportunities at their footstool; but in the end it was his friends children choice of drugs and addictions – that ended up destroying their lives and squashing their chances at maintaining their parent's business and financial legacies by receiving inheritances. Because Trump witnessed this and as a father, he was fixated with preventing his very own kids from going down the same path of destruction. At the time of the writing of this book- Trump's children- all grown up now, have become a major part of their father's company and are successful business people within their own right.

On the flip side of this dynamic, many people are born without family who have money, growing up in a rough environment without the comforts of money, and he/she may not even have the option to inherit money, because their parents or family did not have anything to inherit. Therefore, once they become adults, they may have an unhealthy attachment and an unhealthy view of money. They view money as a way to attain *absolute* happiness, hence tend to develop bad spending habits. With no actual exercise or experience with saving or investing money, these money habits can affect a relationship. Therefore, it is important to first and foremost change how you view money.

The second step is to understand that money do not bring ultimate happiness. Money can buy the means to help make you comfortable. But money cannot bring true happiness. True happiness is attained by an inner peace. Happiness is a state of mind. There are unhappy rich people; and unhappy poor people. Likewise; there are happy rich people and happy poor people.

The next step is to communicate about finances. In an era of plush and lavish extravagant weddings, many couples have turned to loans to pay for their weddings to meet the demands of their dream wedding. I would not suggest this. After the wedding, once everyone departs and are home in their own lives; and newlyweds arrive home from that wedding and honeymoon, you and your spouse will start out in the negative. A negative in finance, can be symbolic to the start of a bad marriage. Going into a marriage with debt can become a serious strain on the newlyweds. Both partners should communicate what is important- the ceremony or the marriage. And at that moment decide and agree on what's best. When planning a wedding it is desired to want your families and friends to be happy and enjoy themselves, but truly it's about the marriage as an entity versus the wedding. Decide what's important and if you are able to finance it on your own, or if you do choose to get a loan — be sure it's manageable and you have a manageable repayment plan.

For relationships, its best to communicate spending styles and establish who is the big spender in the relationship and who is the modest spender. Construct a marital financial plan. Discuss your spending demons with one another in order to construct a plan. Once the plan is set, be committed to that agreement and plan. In the beginning of a relationship discuss any extra debts of payments like student loans, alimony or child support payments that will be paid throughout the relationship.

Practicing spending and shopping self-control is another financial to do when maintaining a lasting love. Ahead of time, while datingwork on your own finances in order to bring something to the table. In our society it is hard to keep up with the daily demands that money will buy. Smartphones and television do not come with antennas anymore, the technology is new and improved. We have to subscribe to some sort of cable or internet Wi-Fi to view online shows, mortgage or rent, car note, insurance and entertainment. The life of today can become quite demanding. And although we can be successful and accomplished with great incomes, let's face it – most of us will not actually become billionaires. And thats okay. But its best to handle money wisely. Therefore, finances should continuously be spent wisely, saved and invested. If there is only one person in the relationship who is the sole breadwinner – this can cause a serious strain and stress on this person. This stress can turn into resentment and anger because they are dealing with the everyday demands of work. Therefore, it is best for both parties to be able to continuously work on the finances and career in order to bring resources to the table to share. If you love someone, you would not want them to become burnt out and emotionally exhausted which can lead to emotional stresses, less sex, less intimacy and other health issues may arise.

Learn when to say no when family and friends or associates ask for money. It is very important to not overcommit yourself. Be sure to communicate with your partner before you give money to someone from any shared bank accounts and finances. Come up with a marital financial system - a system that's tailored to your marriage dynamics. When it comes to spending some couples should have ground rules set in place to what is reasonable to on food per week, spending limits on kid's clothes and toys, and household items. When paying the bills have a system of paying bills, if online or in person, designate if you do this together or agree on which person will do this on their own.

If you ever had a fight about money always understand the basic dynamics and usage of money. If things get to the point of coming close to pulling the plug, consider enlisting the help of a third party who can help you get back on track. For some couples this may be a financial planner, or a church ministry that help with couple's finances. Below is a list of questions to ask your partner while dating, and also answer them yourself in order to gain understanding of money views and money spending habits.

The Money Questions

1. What are some money issues are you unclear about?

2. Do you have debt?

3. Are you organized with money?

4. Are you generous with money?

5. How does your family view money?

6. What are your financial goals in 5 and 10 years from now?

7. Are you a spender or a saver?

8. What is your credit score?

Chapter 23
The Case of the Side Chick

Most of us are familiar with the 80/20 rule. This is essentially the notion that in a healthy relationship, you will receive 80% of what you want from your partner. The remainder 20% are just desires and qualities you are hoping for in the relationship. This theory comes from the general logical notion that no one will ever get 100% of what they want. No person is perfect. Although you may come close, but there is no way anyone can get perfection.

But some men make logic and think - what if I was able to receive and attain both the 80% and the 20 percent? That 20% is generally how the *side chick* is birthed. Now, in a general cheating escapade, the man will generally have one or maybe a couple sexual encounters. The woman he is cheating with may or may not know about the *main chick* or wife. But the difference with the side chick, is that she may very well know about the main chick and is okay with this position and relationship she plays with the man. The main chick may very well know about the side chick or mistress as well, and sometimes they may cross paths to argue and fight.

Now, it is important to note that the side chick is not a necessity for all men. There are some men who are very well happy with their 80% and take that with all pride and happiness. However, unfortunately, many men will admit that they have done so or currently have a woman on the side.

The main chick is someone he trust, love, admire and adore. He generally spends most of his time with her. His family and friends regard her and accept her as his partner. He is comfortable with her and he confides in her. However, the common mistake made by the main chick is that she has became too comfortable with her man. She became lazy in the relationship after a while, as she no long does the things she once did to make her man happy. She may have also slacked on her appearance, may have become nagging, selfish, or always on edge - never smiling anymore. Now once the relationship becomes stressful the man then begins to yearn for a getaway vacation from the relationship. And this is where the side chick comes into the picture. The side chick is his escape, she listens to his marital or main chick problems as he vent, she may cook, clean do whatever he needs her to do. Keep in mind some side chicks are not aware of a girlfriend or a wife. But the difference is that he is not committed to side chick as he is with his main chick or wife. If she know that there is a wife, the side chick is completely okay with playing the "side chick" or "the other woman" role. She can care less about being the main chick because in essence she is not looking for anything serious herself. She is totally fine with having ongoing casual sex and hanging out with no serious emotional attachment. She is ok with just letting the good times roll.

Now this paradox of the side chick is becoming a fad amongst the love and relationships arena and most people have misconceptions which leads other people to jump to attack the side chick and the man as the one who is at fault, and they feel compassion only for the main chick. But in all reality, *all* parties are just as wrong. The argument is that the two people who is having all the fun - the man and his side chick, all the while, while the main chick is there alone. Also there is a common misconception that a man could not love a woman he cheats on. This assumption is not accurate. Men love differently than women. When a man cheat normally it is strictly for physical satisfaction, he still loves his wife but just sexually attracted to another. Men can have sex without being emotionally attached. On the other hand, women in relationships can be attracted to other men as well, however the emotional attachments generally keep a woman from acting on her sexual impulses as much. This is in no way advocating men who cheat but it is important to understand some fundamental differences as explained in the Introduction and previous Chapters of this book.

As mentioned before, all three parties are affected and I will explain. The man is one of the parties who is the major root cause of the problem. Because of his lack of communication to his main partner, he has caused this issue of having the side chick. He chose to bring her into his love triangle. It is important for men to communicate the issues that they are experiencing with their wife. If the wife or partner is hard to talk to and is very emotional, it is best to go to a session of couples counseling to address these issues. Maybe the man stopped "dating" his main partner and has caused her to feel unappreciated and frustrated. Having a side chick will not make the relationship better or stop the issues that they have. It is a façade to a quick fix remedy or make him feel good for the time being. He must also know that his main chick is a woman and should be handled as a delicate flower. It takes perserverance, patience and time. If you decided to commit into a relationship and/or marriage, then this is the responsibility you should take in order to maintain it.

The main partner or wife is the other party who is the other major root cause of the problem. She became relaxed in her relationship and took her man for granted. She began to nag, and stopped adorning herself. She stopped doing all the things she did in the beginning of the relationship. It is important to know that no man is a goldfish where you caught and brought him from the pet store and stored him in a fish tank to reside-swim and swim, until you decide to maintain and clean the water. He is a human being with feelings and possess a heart and need to be treated as such. Treat him as a king that he is. To be encouraged, complimented and nurtured.

Both parties, the man and main woman or wife should both recognize early dynamics that brew the perfect recipe for any form of cheating. Communication, intimacy, trust and control issues are some to name a few. Both parties should strive to make things better in that relationship. If there is room for salvaging the relationship after such broken trust caused by the infidelity, as a last resort, a good therapist can possibly help parties understand what went wrong and then help plan a reconciliation plan for the future.

The side chick is the one party who ideally lose the most. Although some men leave their main chicks and/or families for her, seldom do this happen which leaves the side chick all alone in the end.

Unfortunately, many women out in the world are hurt and damaged from past relationships. They use a wall to protect themselves from any more hurt and pain. They promise to never allow anyone close to their heart to get hurt again. But in reality this is not true because many women in side chick positions still become emotionally attached in an unhealthy way. Women who are settling as a side chick must know that if you want to truly hold a high place in a man's life and to his heart, you have to provide more than just good looks, sex and fun.

Low-self-esteem is the main root reasons for accepting the role as a side chick. Side chicks must know you deserve more for herself than someone else's seconds. Maybe you believed a lie and is telling yourself that you cannot get any man better or no men will deal with you. It's important to get through any lingering issues and know your worth as a woman and embracing this worth would ultimately make you not accept the role as the *side chick*.

Chapter 24
Life is a Risk and So is Love

Risk is around us every day of the week and 24/7. Walking outside of the house, driving, sleeping, even eating — all the things we do in order to survive have some degree of risk involved. It involves some level of danger. So why do we fear risking a shot at healthy love?

Couples must know that being together will involve a risk, however, that risk of healthy long lasting love is worth taking. There is no love without taking a risk. Yes, you have to remember to keep a positive outlook because in the end, you can receive a high return on your investment — a life partner! Love is worth the risk. Everyone must know that risking at love is the only way to attain a healthy love. We can avoid the heartache and pain of possible break up, the in-law differences, the aggrevation of live-in habits like the toilet seat up or down; snoring or farting — all of the marriage or long term relationship aggrevations can be avoided, but for a healthy love, taking a risk is a must.

Start Slow and Build the Love Momentum

I remember having a talk with my business mentor, the late Earlene Wandrey many years ago, and during the talk she said something that always stuck in my head. She said when you meet a man sparks and flames are not good. She said it cannot grow beyond that capacity as it is already at its full capacity. However, when you meet someone and there is a smaller flame, it can grow if you nurture it. In essence what I took from this was that a larger flame would indicate less potential for long term lasting love in a relationship. After all, a flame at its peak will only go out from there. A smaller flame has the potential and space to grow over time, it may not be bright at the moment but with steadier and more consistent – has the potential to become brighter and last much longer as well.

Speaking to those who are already in a loving and stable marriage and relationship, they will most likely say that the feelings they felt when they met their loves were unlike any other feeling that they felt in their past relationships. So if you are still looking for that love, keep an open mind and heart, because the feelings you may experience when you meet someone may not be initially exciting, especially if you are used to feeling those huge sparks. But try to notice if you feel more comfortable and at peace with the person, as if you do not have to put up a front or be someone else. Also notice if this person inspires you to be yourself and the best you can be.

Everyone has a unique experience when they meet their love. However, there is a real sense of coming home. Keeping in mind that a different kind of relationship will feel different from the rest of the other relationships that came before, so if you feel this way, then you may have something unique. Your ultimate goal is not to fall in love. It is to *grow in love*.

Chapter 25
Your Relationship Personality

Over the years in my marriage, my husband and I identified our marriage relationship personality. I could say it's a marriage that have the ingredients of - unconditional love, sharing, great humor, constantly evolving, exploration through traveling and meeting many people from different backgrounds, and also being brutally honest with one another..and more. To further explain relationship or marriage personality, I will use myself as an example - my husband comes from the school of thought where a man may not buy flowers or candy to show your love. He was raised to show love through actions. Not that he gets off the hook for not buying flowers, sometimes he does. But I understand that's not how he operates, he tends to prefer to show his love through real genuine actions. Knowing this about my husband and how it relates to our relationship personality, I am less likely to be influenced, become jealous or unhappy if I see a friend or associate of mine whose husband brought her flowers. I know that my husband loves me and has shown me this in his own way. That our relationship personality does not always involve roses and flowers to define his love. As long as the personality differences is from a healthy place and hold to your shared moral values, then there is no right or wrong personality. It is what works for you both.

Knowing your own relationship personality that includes likes, hobbies and things that fundamentally glue you together as a couple is what's important in order to maintain a lasting healthy love. The whole theme of this concept is to understand your own relationship personality and to identify it so you will be less likely to compare your marriage and relationship to other marriages and relationships. Comparisons can cause serious problems in relationships and can create unwanted desires and resentment for some of the things that others may have or may not have. Keeping in mind that sometimes what you see in other relationships may not always a reality to what is actually happening.

As the relationship progress and grow over the years, I believe every relationship or marriage have to take a pause and continuously identify their own relationship personality. It is almost like a mission statement. These are personality attributes, hobbies and preferences that allow us to connect well and build a deep connection and friendship that is customized to each couple. It also includes compromises. Every couple will have a different set of relationship personality traits customized for their relationship. Knowing this will keep the relationship in perspective and to prevent comparing your marriage and relationship to others. Which is not good. The following is the steps you can take to identify your marriage relationship personality.

How to Identify your Relationship Personality

1. What are some hobbies, activities and events (volunteer, dining, sports, traveling, piano and etc.) you and your mate enjoy doing together? Also list things you choose not to do together that some other couples traditionally do.

2. List common world views, political ideas and social topics you both share in common.

3. List some of the kind gestures (buy flowers, cooks well and etc.) that each person like to do for one another.

4. Write down some things you want your partner to do for you. Decide if this is doable and within reason. Keep a note of this for a later reference to go back to.

5. List the personality traits (have inside jokes only to know about with each other, hardworking, trustworthy and etc.) that your partner said he/she love about you. List the personality traits you love about your partner.

Once you list them out, you will develop your own customized relationship personality, which is like a mission statement. Every now and then refer to the list and make updates if needed. The ultimate goal is to know what each other brings to the table, to make one another happy without comparing your relationship to others.

Chapter 26
Recycle

Nothing is perfect and no one is perfect. Therefore, there is no such thing as a fairytale happily ever after marriage or relationship. This is the misconception. Many people believe that once you find that love or "get a ring", that the hard work is over, and everything will just fall in place. This is a **seriously** common misconception and because of this, causes disappointments.

New found love is easy because it is new, fresh, exciting, and exhilarating. But overtime many couples find it hard to maintain a love at a certain point in the relationship. In logical reality, we cannot expect a great relationship to be smooth-sailing all the way through. We do not live in a perfect world. There will be rocky and turbulent terrains to pass. In this chapter, I will be addressing some simple and proven methods for couples to keep their love going. Maintaining love is a constant vehicle that should be exercised. *If it aint broke don't fix it. Just recycle it!* Recycle the amazing things you do to keep the amazingly healthy the love flowing. The idea is to fall in love over and over again.

Master The Art of Trust and Respect

The problem with the lack of trust in relationships is that couples always focus on trust as it relates to being faithful/cheating to one another. But trust encompasses so much more than being faithful. All relationships are built on trust. By definition, trust is someone's true intentions. Without trust, there can be no healthy relationship. Learning to say no sometimes; being honest with your wants and needs; support your spouse with his/her endeavors; protect your spouse from anyone speaking negative; having empathy for anything your partner or spouse maybe going through and lastly, your word is your bond – are all example scenarios that build trust.

In regards to respect, respect is defined as a deep admiration for someone and by their abilities, qualities and achievements. Respecting your partner will take the relationship far and beyond. Ways to show respect to your partner is to remember to express simple everyday manners – which can easily be forgotten when you're with someone for a while. A simple "please" or "thank you" with a simple nice gesture of appreciation will help your partner or spouse feel respected, loved, appreciated and not taken for granted. Being polite and considerate to one another is another simple way to always maintain the respect.

Master the Art of Variety

Many studies have shown that relationship boredom and dullness almost always lead to dissatisfaction in the relationship. And dissatisfaction sometimes cause infidelities. To prevent this, mastering the art of variety by spicing things up and doing something fun is a great way to keep you and your partner from being bored and dissatisfied. Trying a new restaurant or traveling together can be relationship reinvigorating. Sending a random penis or vagina flirty picture text while he or she is at work can be exciting and spontaneous. Try different things in the bedroom. Switch up your hair style, color or haircut. Add a body piercing. Add a tattoo. Switch up your perfume or cologne. Get a couple of new items to update your wardrobe. As long as you and your partner are ok with it, the varieties are endless. New experiences is key and can help preserve and maintain the closeness and love in their relationship.

Master The Art of Communication

Relationships are not easy. They live and die not by the sword, but by the amount of talk and discussion. It requires work. If two people cannot find a way to openly and honestly communicate their needs, wants and feelings to one another, the relationship does not stand a chance to last in the long term. Effective and efficient communication is one of the top five most important dynamics in order for a relationship to survive.

In order to maintain, couples must find a way to communicate regularly, openly and directly. This does not mean waiting for an argument to ensue in order to tell your spouse how you feel about something that has been bothering you especially with something as small as leaving the toilet seat up or down. It is important to express your feelings as you go along when you feel the need to, and not sweeping your concerns under the rug. When communicating remember to never hit below the belt or make insults. This will only make things worse and may cause a huge argument and later on, resentment and anger. No one can read minds, no matter how long you been in the relationship or know how long you know your spouse and love. Ladies, he doesn't know how you feel, and men, she doesn't know how you feel as well. It has to be expressed and never assumed how each other feel, no matter how long you been together.

Understanding the fundamental differences in men and woman – as discussed in the Introduction and Chapter 3 can help you and your partner understand the differences in how both sexes communicate differently.

Master The Art of Space

We all have heard of the phrase, "absence makes the heart grow fonder," and sometimes this is true. Couples looking to maintain a lasting love must know that it is crucial to practice the art of giving each other space. Hanging out with friends and family; having your own interests/hobbies and occasionally having a night out without your partner can help your relationship. Actually at times while hanging out, you may happen to take notes on other couples and receive an "ah ha" moment – as a reminder of your love, you realize what you actually have at home is infact special.

Missing one another will do good for the relationship's soul. It allows both partners to reset their relationship buttons, relate and relax on their own. Once it's time to join one another again, each will feel rejuvenated and miss one another. Constant smothering in a relationship is not good. This dynamic will almost always lead to relationship burnout and boredom. It may also lead to infidelities. Therefore, it is best to practice and master the art of giving one another space early on in the relationship, even when it's going excitingly great.

Abandonment and trust issues may cause a rift in allowing each other to hang out and give space. If this the case, then any issues should be addressed and worked on in the relationship. If you have to work on yourself to become a whole person with better self-esteem, then it's best to address this as well. When two people fall in love, they are transformed from two independent people into two interdependent people with an intimate connection. However, they are still two people.

11 Steps to Attract a Healthy Relationship and Keep It Alive

Many people believe there is a certain way to meet that special someone. Some meeting places include meeting at a bar, online dating, approaching random strangers in public places. But there is no particular set meeting place. It can be anywhere. Your aura and spirit will attract a love. Women, a man would most certainly approach you if he comfortably feels drawn to you. Your feminine body language, your facial expressions, your confidence is like a magnetic force to a good man. And men, you would know by a woman's body language if she a high value woman, and she would naturally draw you in and be attracted to her.

The following "summarizes" this entire book from beginning to end in eleven simple steps to find a true healthy love. Increase your odds at a lifelong companion; to minimize break-ups, divorces and keep that healthy love alive. If you are married and have not followed these steps, it would be beneficial- a great idea to do so in order to give a better understanding and fix some of the problems that may have crept up in your marriage; or to prevent any serious issues from even happening. Follow these steps to attract and keep a healthy love!

1. Be a Whole Person

This is the most important step in attracting a healthy love. It is the area that will determine if you can either attract a love to you or deflect a love away from youself. In being a whole person you address the fundamental issues causing your roadblocks into attracting a healthy love like — trust issues, cheating issues, communication issues and self-esteem issues. You also address issues causing one to push love away from yourself. For those in relationships or marriages, it also keeps your love going. These issues can affect how you view yourself and can ultimately cause you to be uneasy, impatient, have a deluded judgement which can all lead to you being involved in repeated unhealthy relationships. It can also cause you to have commitment issues with unhealthy patterns of jumping from bed to bed or jumping from relationship to relationship.

2. Have Patience in the Process

Remember: Any time and any place! You can meet your love. While working on being whole, it is important to remember to have patience in the process. Anything good takes time. In the meantime, construct a simple relationship goal. For example: *My goal is to meet my love and life partner who is genuine, funny, loyal and warm within two years and be married within four years. Be sure to pay attention to personality qualities.* If you have not met your partner in that set time, don't feel discouraged, he/she is out there getting prepared for you – the stars all have to align.

3. While Single, Complete Personal Goals

While working on being patient in the process of finding love, and allowing love to attract you – commit yourself to completing one to three goals you always wanted to complete. Maybe it is going back to school to get a degree, taking a class, to pick up an extra professional trade, open a business, travel to a different place, learn how to sew or master an instrument. This will make you more interesting and would bring more to the table once you begin dating and once you find your love. Who knows, you may meet your love while completing a goal!

4. Remember It's Okay to Take a Break from Dating

Sometimes it's best to sit back and take a breather from anything you are "continuously" participating in. This prevent burn out and bitterness from dates that may not have gone the way you would have wanted it to go. Do not feel discouraged. If so, refer back to step one and step two.

5. Attract a Healthy Love by being Positive

Surround yourself with like-minded people. Be happy, and be aware of your body language, your facial expressions, your general appearance. Your demeanor should speak the words of positivity and warmth to attract a like-minded love. Someone who is happy can spot another happy individual. And likewise, someone who is a manipulator can spot his/her victim with low self-esteem a mile away. Give off an appearance, aura and demeanor of value and positivity.

6. Don't Rush into Sex

Simply take your time with sex or abstain and do not have sex until marriage. This will prevent mind cloudiness where you ma ybecome confused with great sex and affection for true love. Instead of a time period or amount of dates, if you choose sex, I suggest waiting until you know about your dating partners personality, moral values, views on world topics, have met both, the friends/family and you both went "together" for STDs and HIV testing.

7. Know How to Walk Away from Red Flags

It is best to use your human inherited "gut" instincts to **prevent** hurt, harm or danger in our personal and love lives. It is best to prevent this instead of playing damage control to a unsafe and unhealthy situation you placed yourself in, simply because you decided to take an unwise chance and risk. This is not wise, because it can be someone very dangerous and the risk can backfire, causing you to sacrifice your life and/or freedom. When we see red flags some of us choose to acknowledge them and avoid the person and some do the opposite. Run, not walk away from red flags. It just best to be safe and not sorry.

8. Put Your Best Foot Forward

For women- when dating you should have fun; smile, be funny, easy going, have a great personality; know current affairs to be able to hold a conversation, tap into your inner feminine woman. All these qualities will lure that amazing man to you and also keep him interested. For men, when dating - have fun, be spontaneous, be cordial, give off a strong leadership aura, have a great conversation, be easy going and don't expect perfection. For both men and women – play up your physical features forget that you are a short man or a woman with few extra pounds, confidence is key. If you have an amazing walk, walk! If you have amazing legs or lips, work that! Feel your strength and your confidence through your assets. Know that no one person is perfect, even the individuals that you think is perfect, have some complaints about themselves. So just do you!

9. Be Friends

Friendship is an important dynamic for long term and lasting love. Be one another's best friend. Don't just date, be friends! Talk, laugh, do activities together, travel together, and expect growth in the relationship.

10. Understand that the More You Give, the More You Receive

I think this is one the most misunderstood dynamic. Inspirational author, Orison Marden said "We must give more in order to get more. It is the generous giving of ourselves that produces the generous harvest." He sums it up well. Some people are not receiving a healthy love they deserve, because they are not giving love. Love is not selfish. Give love. It can be love around you in the world we live in, in our society. Also this doesn't mean paying for all the dates or giving money to your date. What it's about is giving in the relationship; giving time, effort, commitment, self-control, loyalty, giving your heart and understanding. Give these qualities it to someone *deserving* of it, in other words – you are planting seeds in fertile ground, and later you will be able to enjoy the harvest of healthy fruit.

11. Learn to Master the Art of Reinvention and Recycling

At this stage you would have successfully attracted and found a healthy love. Congratulations! Now it is time to repeat the previous steps. Love and relationships requires constant - continuous attention of nurturing for it to last long term. It is important to remember that what may work in the beginning may not work after three years of a relationship. Never allow your love flame to wither and die out. Sometimes you have to reinvent your marriage relationship; constantly recycling the concepts that help it flourish. If you commit to love, love will commit to you.

Acknowledgements

I thank my husband, Obinna for showing me an unconditional love and an amazing love journey that has inspired me to write this book. You are the essence of my healthy love. Many thanks to my editor Ruth Bell. Thank for your hard work.
I thank my Uncle Jeffrey Monk. I remember and thank the late – my dad Alton Galloway, Uncle Tyrone Monk and Uncle Alfonso Hollimon. Men in my life who protected me and imparted the wisdom in me as a young girl. You may not know how much wisdom you gave me on how a man should treat a woman. Thanks to my cousin John King for your love and protection. All my male family members who love and respect me over the years. It is because the love you all have shown me that made me the woman I am today. You are all true men. I also thank my mother, Cheryl who always in parted wisdom in my life. Thank my grandmother, Ada who is the epitome of a feminine woman. I would like to thank all the people who I have been inspired by through experiences or through witnesses. I thank my entire family, and friends - Jamaal, Tequin, Jamillah, Rashedah, Deidra, Abdulrahman, Andrae the remainder of all my amazing close friends, family, colleagues and professional connections. God bless you. I love you all.

About the Author

BAYYINAH MONK-NDUAKA'S THIRD BOOK, *Gimme Some Relationship Advice! How to Find Love and Keep* She is the author of the best-selling cookbooks Gimme That Recipe! and Gimme That Smoothie Recipe! which were Amazon #1 best seller for three consecutive weeks. An avid writer, Bayyinah began writing poetry and prose at the age of 12 and while in junior high school excelled on advanced placement reading and writing courses throughout. She is a 1995 alumna of Young Writer's at Kenyon College. A graduate of Otterbein University and Briarwood College (now Lincoln College of New England), Bayyinah wears many professional hats as a funeral mortuary professional, business consultant, caterer as well as an author.